HORSERACING

David Ashforth

Hammersley House
5-8 Warwick Street
London W1B 5LX
United Kingdom

Email: info@bluffers.com
Website: bluffers.com
Twitter: @BluffersGuide

First published 2015
Copyright © Bluffer's® 2015

Publisher: Thomas Drewry
Managing Director: Sarah Clegg
Publishing Director: Brooke McDonald

Series Editor: David Allsop
Design and Illustration: Jim Shannon

ISBN: 978-1-909937-36-9 (print)
       978-1-909937-37-6 (ePub)
       978-1-909937-38-3 (Kindle)

CONTENTS

'I'd rather have a goddam horse.
A horse is at least human, for God's sake.'

JD Salinger, *The Catcher in the Rye*

THE START

Chasing foxes and servants can only keep a man entertained for so long. During the late eighteenth century, with no French Revolution to remove their heads and duels falling out of favour, English aristocrats increasingly occupied themselves by seeing whose horse was the fastest.

Speed was of the essence and, by mating their mares with exotic imported stallions – namely the Byerley Turk, the Darley Arabian and the Godolphin Arabian – aristocrats found themselves galloping faster and faster. Eventually, in 1780, they reached Derby.

They would have reached Bunbury but when the Earl of Derby and Sir Charles Bunbury tossed a coin to decide what to call a new race, at Epsom, Derby won. Over a century later, if Bunbury had still been alive (he wasn't) he might have been consoled by his appearance in Oscar Wilde's *The Importance of Being Earnest*. As it was, he was consoled by winning the first Derby with a handsome chestnut called Diomed.

The important thing to remember is that every

thoroughbred horseracing today is a descendant of either the Byerley Turk, the Darley Arabian or the Godolphin Arabian. The bluffer might usefully, and nonchalantly, remark, 'Of course, there isn't really much difference between any of them. They all come from the same three stallions, historically.'

This should be enough to spark off any attendant bloodstock expert and, while he or she delivers a long and complicated monologue, all that is required of the bluffer is to adopt a knowing and superior air, nodding occasionally.

THE HEART OF THE MATTER

If a horse seems to have a lot of body near the front, it is worth speculating in approving terms on the likely size of its heart and lungs. Just as a car with a 2000cc engine is more powerful than a 1000cc version, so the size of a racehorse's heart affects its performance.

A big heart, known in racing as 'an engine', is a good thing. The two greatest Flat racehorses, arguably of all time (because there's always an argument), Secretariat and Frankel, both had exceptionally large hearts. Secretariat's heart weighed about 21lbs, well over double the average. Like Frankel, he had 'a tremendous engine'.

Yet, with a racehorse, the heart of the matter is not so much the heart as the legs. It doesn't take a degree in anatomy to figure out that they have a fundamental design flaw.

Having started off, in the proverbial mists of time, with five toes on each foot, the thoroughbred somehow managed to lose four of them, leaving it with only its middle toe to stand on. If that isn't bad enough, it has ridiculously thin legs.

Whereas most creatures use their legs to move around, the thoroughbred racehorse uses his to give sleepless nights to his owner and trainer, and a lucrative occupation to members of the veterinary profession. The expression, 'He's got a leg,' although at first sight both obvious and reassuring, upon closer examination turns out to be shorthand for 'He's got a leg but it's got something wrong with it. I haven't looked at the other three yet.'

The bluffer will always be on sound ground when asking, 'How are his legs?' The same thought will have occupied most of the trainer's waking hours since he was first issued with a licence. During brief intervals when the trainer is not worrying about his horses' legs, he is feeling them, because he knows they can't be trusted. No trainer's wife has as much attention paid to her legs, however fine, as the most knock-kneed horse in the yard does.

If the legs in question are fine and dandy today, they are only one false step away from being put in the care of a veterinary surgeon for the next month. Wherever a stone is to be found, a racehorse can be relied upon to seek it out and step on it.

At heart, the thoroughbred is a collection of parts which, when working in harmony, present one of the finest sights known to man. It is a pity that they are most in harmony when the horse is standing still.

Wonderful though the thoroughbred racehorse is, it has

an unfortunate predisposition to commit suicide, with the occasional murder thrown in. Even in its stable, it cannot be relied upon not to self-harm, being prone to be 'cast in its box', meaning that it is lying down and either can't or won't get up. This may be because he is due to race at three o'clock that afternoon at Catterick, or because he has got stuck. When you try to help him up, he is liable to injure both himself and you. Someone else will have to call the

---

♛

Wherever a stone is to be found,
a racehorse can be relied upon
to seek it out and step on it.

---

doctor and the vet. As the horse is more highly valued than his trainer, the first call will be to the vet, whose bill will be bigger than the doctor's, with more scans and sophisticated treatment to be arranged.

Obviously, things become more dangerous when a racehorse emerges from its box. In the outside world, the opportunities for mayhem are almost infinite. Suffice it to say that if an outing to either the gallops or a racecourse is completed with both horses and humans intact, it has been a good day, and an unusual one. The trainer might even get a decent night's sleep.

He or she will need it, because tomorrow the horse will probably have 'got a leg'.

That is why one of the most admired features of a racehorse is its ears. Not only is it rarely necessary to summon a vet to examine a horse's ears but, pricked up and alert, they give a horse's head a noble air. The horse stands there, staring into the distance, ears erect, a magnificent sight, ready to be photographed. When it puts its ears down, it means that the photographer is about to be bitten.

If you still think you'd like to own one, it's time you trotted along to the sales. More on this later.

WHAT THIS BOOK WILL DO FOR YOU

Horseracing is a maze. People have spent lifetimes trying to find their way around it, even out of it. The bluffer hasn't got a lifetime to spare and, when he finds himself on the spot, this short but definitive guide offers invaluable help.

It sets out to conduct you through the main danger zones encountered in discussions about horseracing and to equip you with the vocabulary and evasive technique that will minimise the risk of being rumbled as a bluffer. It will give you a few easy-to-learn hints and techniques that might even allow you to be accepted as a horseracing expert of rare ability and experience. But it will do more.

It will give you the tools to impress legions of marvelling listeners with your knowledge and insight – without anyone discovering that, until you read this, you probably didn't know the difference between a handicap and a hurdle.

'He'd better be good.'

Demi O'Byrne, after bidding
$16 million for The Green Monkey

IS THAT A BID, SIR?

Imagine that you are Alice, the one in *Alice's Adventures in Wonderland,* and have just fallen down a rabbit hole, emerging to find yourself in a strange land full of strange creatures and strange happenings. The land is divided into territories, with names such as Tattersalls, Goffs and Keeneland. You have entered the fantasy world of bloodstock sales. A strange word, bloodstock. A strange word in a strange land.

Alice was probably not dressed for the bloodstock sales, and you should not dress over-smartly yourself. If jeans are good enough for Sheikh Mohammed, ruler of Dubai and the biggest racehorse-owner in the world, then they are ideal for you. No suit, no tie, no outward sign that you are an enormously wealthy big player, or could be if a horse appeared that merited the attention of your discerning eye.

The bluffer will need a sales catalogue to clutch and examine studiously, and a pad of small yellow sticky labels. Place the labels at intervals throughout the catalogue, so that they poke out intriguingly from the edges of the pages. Then write notes on the labels and pages. 'Two pints of semi-skimmed milk', 'cough mixture', 'fetlocks?', '£400,000 max'. That sort of thing.

At Keeneland, a beautiful venue in Kentucky, USA, blessed with lovely trees and birds, vendors with their yearlings (horses in the calendar year after the year of their birth) stabled in the barns supply drinks and snacks while you express interest in Hip (alias the lot number worn on its hip) 345. You ask to see the horse and stare intently as it is trotted up and down. Write a few more notes in your catalogue: 'big bum', 'white blaze on nose not straight', 'excellent cookies'.

At Tattersalls, in Newmarket, it is worth leaning against the railings as the horses are walked around behind the sales ring, ready to enter it. Each horse's lot number is displayed on a label stuck to the horse's backside, a bit like an apple in a grocery store, but more expensive and less popular for eating.

A knowledgeable look is the main requirement for the bluffer, perhaps reinforced by the occasional mutter: 'long pasterns', 'short back', 'over at the knee'. There are several horses walking round, so the chances are that at least one of the things you say will be right. With horses, so much is a matter of opinion. The bluffer is always of the opinion that his opinion is a match for anyone else's. After all, some of the most respected bloodstock agents in the world have chosen some real turkeys, which is what they might as well have been.

Many's the horse bought for 150,000 guineas as a yearling and sold, several slow runs and many thousands of pounds in training fees later, for 1,500 guineas. The agent, as well as taking five per cent in commission, takes such setbacks bravely in his stride, asking his client, 'Are you game for another go, sir? Only I've just seen a lovely Oasis Dream, and I think we might get her for 300,000.'

That's what they say when describing a horse: an 'Oasis Dream', a 'Galileo', a 'Montjeu'. If Catherine, Duchess of Cambridge, appeared at Tattersalls (she probably won't), they'd say she was a Michael Middleton.

THE ART OF BIDDING

In *Alice's Adventures in Wonderland*, there is the Mad Hatter. In the sales ring, there is the Mad Auctioneer, waving his hammer. At Tattersalls it goes something like this:

> *Who will give me 300? A tremendous filly. I'm selling now. You wouldn't want to miss out on this. Thank you, sir. Do I have 350? 350 it is and you won't regret it. Round it off now at 400. Well done, sir.*

(That's 400,000 guineas, or £420,000 in the real world.)

At Keeneland it might go more like this:

> *500 now, who'll give me 50 more for the Giant's Causeway? Texas gentleman 575, oh he's good. Who's going to help me? Help yourself too, at 700.*

(That's $700,000.)

Not that $700,000 is worth paying much attention to. Clapping doesn't start until $1 million, proper clapping until $2 million, and a bit of cheering to go with the clapping at $4 million.

There's the horse; there's the man cleaning up behind the horse; there are the bid spotters, spotting bids; and there are the bidders, bidding for themselves; and then there are the agents, bidding for others, with their money. No one waves his arms and shouts, 'Cooeee, over here!' It's just a blink of the eye, a nod of the chin, a flick of the catalogue, a poker player's flat face.

At the yearling sales, egos and empires collide to periodically produce gripping eruptions, during which the law of demand and supply, particularly demand, puts up a spectacular display while the law of diminishing returns is ejected from the building.

That's the law that states, roughly speaking, that if you pay $4 million for a yearling rather than $2 million, the extra $2 million will barely improve the chances of it being able to run fast. Not that a million or two is worth fussing over.

Famously, at Keeneland in 1983, Sheikh Mohammed paid $10.2 million for Snaafi Dancer. Sent to trainer John Dunlop, Snaafi Dancer proved too slow to race. Sent to stud, he proved too infertile to be persisted with. He was discreetly retired to a farm in Florida.

Fortunately for Sheikh Mohammed, in 2006 he lost a bidding battle with Coolmore, John Magnier's Irish breeding and racing empire, for the right to own The Green Monkey, an unraced two-year-old who had shown himself to be very fast over one furlong (a furlong is 220 yards, an eighth of a mile). Unfortunately, there aren't any races over one furlong.

Demi O'Byrne, in the Magnier corner, and John Ferguson, in the Sheikh Mohammed corner, slugged it out until, finally, O'Byrne made the winning bid of $16 million. Randy Hartley and Dean De Renzo were pleased. Seven months earlier, they had bought the colt as a yearling for $425,000.

Sadly, $16 million turned out to be about $16 million more than The Green Monkey was worth. Injured in training, he finally appeared on a racetrack as a three-year-old in 2007, but after losing three times, for which he earned $10,440, he was retired to stud in Florida, where he is available for sexual services for the modest fee of $5,000. He's not complaining.

Buying multimillion-dollar, or -pound, yearlings is likely to be beyond the bluffer's reach, but bidding for them is not. A few investigative probes will establish the lots likely to attract the big hitters and, when the auctioneer invites bids starting at, say, 100,000 guineas, it is time for the bluffer to enter the fray, with a calm wave of his catalogue.

Having entered the fray, the bluffer will quickly leave it, his job done. 'Yes,' the bluffer can confide later, several times, 'I tried to get the Galileo myself, but I was up against Magnier and Sheikh Fahad. He went for 3.6 million, and I wasn't prepared to go quite that far.'

There is always the second-hand sales, officially known as the horses in training sales. They are for horses that someone wanted once but doesn't want anymore.

'A racehorse is an animal that can take several thousand people for a ride at the same time.'

Anon

HOW TO BE AN OWNER

The great beauty of having bought a yearling is that you don't know how bad it will be. In time, it might be another Dancing Brave or Desert Orchid, Arkle or Frankel – and you own it. There is everything to look forward to – Royal Ascot, Glorious Goodwood, the Cheltenham Festival, Wolverhampton.

As the bluffer might say, 'Yes, I own racehorses. As a matter of fact, I was at the sales last month. We picked up a Pivotal*. We're very hopeful.'

The 'we' might be the royal 'we', or the bluffer and his partner, or the bluffer and several scores of strangers united in an ownership syndicate.

Hope springs eternal but, just in case, it's best not to test it out too soon. These things take time – months, years, a lifetime. With racehorses, patience is a virtue to be embraced. As long as there is patience, there is hope.

Your pride and joy needs to live somewhere and, as you don't have a suitable spare bedroom, or paddock, and need

---

* *See* previous chapter re: Duchess of Cambridge.

to abide by the rules of racing, he will have to be sent to a licensed trainer and given a name, and vet's bills. 'The Bluffer' sounds splendid and a lot more appealing than many of the bizarre names racehorses have been lumbered with.

A horse is obviously not a Squirrel, Seagull, Arctic Penguin, Snow Leopard or March Hare, except in the eyes of the owners who bestowed those names upon them. At least they share warm blood, unlike the Bayonet, Metal Detector and Chandelier allotted to other racehorses. Then there is the unlikely sight of Mango Chutney, Peach Sorbet and Chocolate Cake galloping into view.

Racehorses have been named after places, such as Marble Arch and Istanbul, and after people, including Lawrence Of Arabia and Ned Kelly. It's difficult to imagine Oscar Wilde leaping over an open ditch, but he has done, as have Elgar and the Duke Of Buckingham. During the early 2000s, a Harlot and an Archbishop were both racing in Britain, although never in the same race, which was perhaps just as well. They would have made uneasy bedfellows.

There have been some very clever names, and some rather naughty ones, like Passing Wind, which didn't stop him winning a hurdle race at Bangor in 2001 and a chase at Fakenham two years later.

A horse whose sire was Busted and whose dam was Amazer gloried in the name of Amazing Bust. Busted was named for trouble. Another of his children, out of Divided, was called Cleavage. Cleverer still were Rhett Butler, by Bold Lad out of Pussy Galore, and Entire, a gelding out of Tactless.

One of the cleverest of all was conjured up by the late Louis Freedman, owner of Cliveden Stud. In 1973, he had a yearling filly by Reform out of Seventh Bride, and named her One Over Parr. Catherine Parr was Henry VIII's sixth wife.

Still, nobody likes a clever clogs. The Bluffer will be fine. So that's decided. Now, who should train him?

YOUR TRAINER

The correct choice of trainer is vital. Some trainers only train Flat horses while others train only jumpers. Some train both. Some trainers are very good while others are very hopeless.

The bluffer may find it attractive to have The Bluffer educated by a member of the aristocracy, such as Sir Mark Prescott or Sir Michael Stoute, both fine trainers, based in Newmarket, the headquarters of British racing. Selecting them would offer the opportunity to remark, casually, 'As I was saying to Sir Michael the other day,' or 'Sir Mark was telling me,' or even, 'Evidently the Queen took a liking to my filly at Sir Michael's.'

The size of ponds and fishes is worth bearing in mind. At leading Flat trainer Mark Johnston's yard, at Middleham in North Yorkshire, you would be a small fish in a large pond, much of it taken up by Sheikh Hamdan bin Mohammed al Maktoum's enormous collection of racehorses. Similarly, at leading jumps trainer Nicky Henderson's yard, at Upper Lambourn in Berkshire, you would be a minnow swimming with sharks, or friendlier aquatics, with names such as JP McManus, Robert Waley-Cohen and Simon Munir.

On the other hand, McManus is a noted gambler and the bluffer could then find himself saying, 'I was talking to JP at Nicky's the other day. He was telling me about one they've laid out for a handicap at the Cheltenham Festival. I've taken 16-1. Love to bring you in on it but mum's the word, I'm afraid.' At this point, a gentle tap on the side of your nose wouldn't go amiss.

McManus's racing colours, green and gold hoops, are instantly recognisable and your choice of colours should be made carefully – striking, yet dignified. A set of exclamation marks on luminous pink silks, with a flashing bobble on the cap, perhaps. Since that wouldn't be allowed, at least instruct your trainer that The Bluffer should always wear a sheepskin noseband, for ease of recognition. Otherwise you might have to tell the jockey to wave every now and again to let you know where he is, which would be silly.

Unlike paint, horses are only available in a small range of colours, notably bay, brown, chestnut and grey, with black making rare appearances and white even rarer ones, in the form of Mont Blanc II (foaled 1963) and Russe Blanc (foaled 2007).

While white has the virtue of standing out from the crowd, as Russe Blanc's trainer Richard Lee once pointed out, it takes an awful lot of cleaning. That is worth bearing in mind. Not that you'll be doing the cleaning.

WHICH ONE'S MINE?

Since – a rather alarming fact – most racehorses never win a race in their lives, watching their pre-race performances on the gallops has a lot to recommend it. They don't get beaten as often there.

Visiting your trainer's yard is one of the most enjoyable parts of racehorse ownership, although it is not without its hazards. On your first visit, you will notice that most of the horses look the same. If the runners for this year's Derby were secretly exchanged for a collection of humble selling platers, most of the crowd would not notice the difference, so there is no shame in asking, which one's mine?

Most racehorses never win a race in their lives.

As your trainer introduces you to The Bluffer, who will show no sign of either recognition, interest or gratitude, he will explain some of the fundamentals. The Bluffer will have had the virus, and probably ringworm. He will recently have been scoped, which involves sticking a tube down the horse's throat to collect samples, to confirm that he has, indeed, got an infection. That is why he has yet to make his debut on the gallops. If he has managed a bit of exercise, he will have sore shins. Either way, a vet's bill will be on its way shortly.

Under the circumstances, it may be best not to say, 'He's looking well, isn't he?' A safer option would be, 'He's grown since the sales, hasn't he?' or 'He's still a bay, then?'

Once he is well enough, about halfway through the season,

you will be able to watch him on the gallops. By this time, your trainer will have something to report, namely, 'He's done nothing wrong.' This is a popular expression among trainers and is good news. It means that, although The Bluffer has done nothing worthy of positive note, he has not yet killed either himself or his rider. Hope remains intact.

When The Bluffer is safely back in his box, you can expect to be offered a hearty breakfast of the kind never recommended in guidebooks for healthy living and delayed dying. Bacon, sausages, eggs, buttered toast and marmalade, that kind of thing. Eat it all. It may be the most valuable thing you have to show for your 'investment'.

FOLLOWING PROGRESS

Trainers often situate their stables in remote rural areas, as far from their owners as possible. You can't visit them every day, or even every week, so it will be necessary to phone your trainer regularly to hear the latest news of The Bluffer's progress, if any. Trainers can be troublesome about this, possibly pointing out that you are not their only owner and they are busy people. Nowadays, they may even operate a website and write blogs telling all and sundry about your horse. It is worth repeating the last bit. Your horse. Well, yours and the other members of the 40-member partnership.

Trainers are, indeed, busy people and it is best to establish a pattern of communication. Phone daily or every other day at the same time. 11.00pm is a good time because the work of the day will be over and the trainer will probably not be on the phone to anyone else.

Although you are trying to be accommodating, you may not receive the appreciation you deserve. Dorothy Paget, who owned the mighty Golden Miller, winner of the Cheltenham Gold Cup five times and the Grand National once, in 1934, liked to ring her trainers at about midnight and talk for a long time. Once, when a desperate Basil Briscoe took his phone off the hook, Paget sent a messenger at 2.30am, ordering the trainer to replace it.

'Training horses is child's play,' Briscoe once remarked, 'but it's a hell of a bloody job trying to train Miss Paget.'

Many years later, champion jumps trainer Fulke Walwyn imposed a 9.00pm limit on Miss Paget's calls but, describing her as 'so trying', still eventually resigned as her trainer.

Obviously, Briscoe and Walwyn were at fault in not going to bed later and you should not be deterred by the poor example they set. Remind yourself and, if necessary, your trainer, of the admirable saying, 'He who pays the piper calls the tune.' Exactly.

Now and again, you may find it necessary to change trainers. Now and again, your trainer may find it necessary to change owners.

WHAT NEXT?

Once The Bluffer is fit and well, the next step is for the trainer to inform you that your horse is 'not an early type'. This is good news. Early types are flighty, precocious creatures that might sparkle briefly and win a few races but are liable to splutter and fade, their energies soon spent. The Bluffer is made of sterner stuff. He is built to last.

Naturally, his owner will need to be patient. The horse needs time to 'grow into his frame'. This means that he has a large skeleton with lots of room to fill. Only time and an enormous number of breakfasts and dinners will do the job. Reassuringly, The Bluffer has still 'done nothing wrong'. Also, he is 'a good doer', meaning that he is outstanding at eating. Excellent!

Having bought your horse as a yearling, you might hope to see him perform at a racecourse the following year, as a two-year-old. That is until your trainer tells you that 'He will make a three-year-old.' He may still run as a two-year-old but, if he does, don't expect him to run as fast as the others. It's just a warm-up. He needs more time.

Thoroughbreds are strong yet fragile creatures. All sorts of things can go wrong so that, even a horse expected to 'make a three-year-old' may pass his three-year-old season confined largely to his box, occasionally venturing into the indoor school, the swimming pool, the gallops and, perhaps once or twice, to the racecourse. Hopefully, he will make a four-year-old.

WHERE TO GO
AND WHAT TO KNOW

There's a racecourse for everyone, and Britain is blessed with a wonderful variety of them. It's difficult to say exactly how many there are at the moment because they keep opening (Great Leighs, 2008) and closing (Great Leighs, 2009) and then opening again (Chelmsford City, alias Great Leighs, 2015). In 2012, Hereford and Folkestone also closed. If you say there are around 60 racecourses, from Newton Abbot in the south to Perth in the north, you won't be far wrong.

There are various ways of dividing them up. There are racecourses that stage only Flat (no jumps) racing, like Newmarket, courses that stage only jump racing, like Cheltenham, and those that stage both, such as Newbury and Sandown Park. On the Flat, there are all-weather courses with artificial surfaces made from polytrack (Chelmsford City, Kempton and Lingfield), tapeta (Wolverhampton) or fibresand (Southwell), and turf courses (the rest).

There are right-handed tracks, like Musselburgh and Leicester; left-handed tracks, like Haydock and Nottingham; and even figure-of-eight tracks, namely Fontwell Park and Windsor. There are flat tracks, like Yarmouth, and anything but flat tracks, like Towcester. Small, sharp tracks, like Chester, and large galloping ones, like Doncaster.

There are premier division racecourses, such as Aintree, Ascot, Cheltenham and Sandown Park for jump racing, and Ascot, Epsom, Goodwood, Newmarket, Sandown Park and York for the Flat. They are courses that generally provide good facilities and stage valuable, prestige events that attract top-class horses. At the humble end of the spectrum are courses like Southwell, Brighton and Sedgefield, offering relatively small prize money for moderate horses.

Some fixtures, particularly on all-weather tracks, are staged largely for the benefit of the off-course betting industry, with few customers watching at the racecourse but many more in betting shops. Sometimes, that is the best place to watch from, especially in the winter. When there's a cold February twilight meeting at Kempton, there's a warm one in Ladbrokes.

If you've been to one racecourse, you definitely haven't been to them all (fairly obvious, really). Racecourses all offer the sight of jockeys on horses, but a midsummer afternoon at Goodwood is a world apart from a winter jumps meeting at Bangor, which doesn't have a grandstand (Goodwood does, several).

The bluffer, perhaps drawn by his social aspirations to the exclusivity and kudos of Royal Ascot and Glorious Goodwood, may favour them, but the very real delights of Cartmel and Perth, Salisbury and Hamilton, and many other tracks, should not be ignored.

The British Horseracing Authority having given the green light to racing on Good Friday, there is now racing every day of the year except Christmas Day and the two days before it, for shopping. There is an abundance of choice. Where should you go, and when?

ASCOT

If the bluffer wishes to ask, 'Will you be joining me at Royal Ascot this year? I haven't missed one for 20 years, you know,' it might be as well to actually go, after 20 years watching on TV. Obtaining entry to the Royal Enclosure can be difficult, as can obtaining a cup of tea in a proper cup, or for less than about £2.80.

The latter problem can be solved by bringing your own teabags, sequestering a cup, and using the hot-water tap in the toilets; the former either by marrying a member of the royal family or by persuading an existing Royal Enclosure badgeholder, who has attended Royal Ascot at least four times, to sponsor your application. Failing that, a member is allowed to bring two guests on the Friday or Saturday. It is the bluffer's job to be such a guest.

You would miss the Ascot Gold Cup on the Thursday – Ladies Day – which is a shame because the two-and-a-half-mile race offers an excellent opportunity to avoid queuing for the toilet. Then again, so does Saturday's Queen Alexandra Stakes, over almost two and three-quarter miles. Every day at Royal Ascot, held in June, is a good day, whether you want to gawp at other racegoers or at the horses. There are some splendid examples of both.

You will be dressed, of course, in morning dress, unless you are a woman, in which case you will wear an outfit of captivating elegance, including a hat, but not a fascinator (an item no longer welcome in the Royal Enclosure). Men will generally opt for black or grey, perhaps with a daring choice of socks, while women will wear dresses with colours embracing the entire spectrum and hats that have to be seen to be believed. It is best to wear one that doesn't require the full-time services of one of your hands to stop it blowing off.

You are unlikely to see impersonators of the late Linda Lovelace, at least not in the Royal Enclosure. In 1974, the porn star arrived in a silver Rolls-Royce, number plate PEN15, and attempted to enter Ascot's hallowed grounds wearing a see-through blouse. She was foiled by a bowler-hatted gateman and retreated to the bonnet of her car, where she posed for appreciative photographers.

A new £210 million grandstand was opened in 2006, which had the unfortunate consequence of bringing members of the Royal Enclosure into closer proximity with the lower orders than traditionally considered desirable. Seemingly modelled on airport terminals, with enormous escalators and millions of square feet of air, the new building was closed a short while later. It reopened in 2007 with improved viewing in the new grandstand and more toilets added to the Silver Ring Enclosure.

The bluffer may want to pay particular attention to the Royal Procession which precedes each day's racing and to play his part in getting in the way of serious racegoers attempting either to look at the horses in the parade ring or reach a bookmaker in the betting ring.

Champagne, gossip, critiques of other racegoers and name-dropping, laced with occasional references to Frankie Dettori, the darling of the crowd, are very much in order. By 2014, Dettori, now in the veteran stage of a colourful career, had totted up 49 winners at the Royal meeting, not to mention his Magnificent Seven, when Dettori won every race at the non-Royal Ascot meeting on 28 September 1996.

If your audience is not impressed by your knowledge of things Dettori, it might be worth introducing Brown Jack (winner of the Ascot Stakes in 1928 and of the Queen Alexandra Stakes from 1929 to 1934) and Yeats (winner of the Ascot Gold Cup four years in a row, from 2006 to 2009) into the conversation.

There are questions the bluffer might casually yet fruitfully pose, such as, 'Would you say Yeats was a better stayer than Brown Jack? What do you think? I've always thought well of Ardross myself. That run in the Arc was something, wasn't it?'

Ardross was narrowly beaten in the 1982 Prix de l'Arc de Triomphe at Longchamp, having won the Ascot Gold Cup both that year and the previous one. Or you could simply say, 'What does she think she's wearing? With that dress, I can believe everything they say about her.'

Since 2011, Ascot has also been the stage for Qipco British Champions Day, the grand finale for the season's Qipco British Champions Series, which features 35 of the racing calendar's top Flat races. Held in October, British Champions Day offers about £4 million in prize money and the bluffer will not want to miss it. He would not have missed it for the world in 2012, when Frankel ended his magnificent career by winning the Qipco Champion Stakes.

GLORIOUS GOODWOOD

Like Royal Ascot, Glorious Goodwood is a major feature of the social as well as the racing calendar. Pimm's and panama hats are the trademark symbols of the five-day meeting that bridges July and August at one of the most beautiful racecourses in Britain.

♛

'A racecourse should be a place where you would be happy to have a heart attack.'

Michael Turner, former British Horseracing Authority chief medical adviser

---

It is also one of the few racecourses where there is architectural harmony rather than the hotchpotch of buildings that characterise many courses – harmony, elegance and imagination, as seen in the rather fetching white tent-roofed pavilions.

Stand on the grandstand steps and admire the view across the Sussex countryside, with barely a building in sight. Stand by the parade ring and admire the horses, or in a pavilion and admire the champagne and seafood, or in the racecourse betting shop and see what's going on at Redcar. You might need to back a winner there to pay for the exotically priced champagne.

The Sussex Stakes, over a mile, is the high-class highlight of the meeting. Some wonderful horses have won the race, including the mighty Brigadier Gerard in 1971. 40 years later, the equally mighty Frankel was the winner and, uniquely, repeated the feat the following year.

Less elite but also prestigious, the Stewards' Cup, a six-furlong cavalry charge, has been contested since 1840. As you will know, the winner that year was Epirus. It was the only year he won the Cup, a statement also true for every other winner apart from Sky Diver, who won in 1967 and 1968.

The Stewards' Cup, a busy betting race beloved of bookmakers, has been won by some distinguished sprinters, none more worthy than Lochsong. After winning the Cup in 1992, the Ian Balding-trained filly won two of the season's other major sprint handicaps, the Portland Handicap at Doncaster and the Ayr Gold Cup. The following year, as part of a tremendous curriculum vitae, Lochsong won the Nunthorpe Stakes at York and the Prix de l'Abbaye at Longchamp in Paris, a race she won again in 1994. What a horse! – as, no doubt, you exclaimed during your recent conversation with the 10th Duke of Richmond or, as you know him, Charles, the owner of Goodwood racecourse.

CHELTENHAM

Cheltenham is the Mecca of jump racing. Although 3,000 miles apart, both are renowned for attracting a vast number of worshippers. In 2013, over 400,000 racegoers visited Cheltenham, 235,000 of them during the four-day Festival meeting, in March.

Sometimes, every significant jump race during the winter months seems merely to be a starter dish, followed by the bookmakers' revised ante-post prices for the main dishes at the Festival.

The November meeting, with the Paddy Power Gold Cup as its highlight, has grown in stature in recent years, merely confirming Cheltenham's pre-eminence in jump racing. It is a tremendously popular racecourse, unmatched for the anticipation and expectation it generates. People look forward for months to backing the wrong horse in the Cheltenham Gold Cup, which is what almost everyone did in 1990, when Norton's Coin won at 100-1.

The sport's great stars, too many to list, are woven into the Festival's history. Now and again, it behoves the bluffer to remark, while apparently in a dreamlike trance, 'There'll never be another Arkle, will there?'

Universally regarded as the greatest chaser of all time, Arkle won the Gold Cup three times in a row, from 1964 to 1966. Mention of his name never comes amiss. Nor, indeed, that of the charismatic grey, Desert Orchid, who won the Gold Cup in 1989 but was even better elsewhere, winning the King George VI Chase at Kempton four times. 'I loved Dessie,' should do the trick. 'Really loved him ..." (dab your eye, but don't over do it).

If your audience is a younger one, try mentioning Big Buck's, winner of the World Hurdle from 2009 to 2012. If that fails to elicit the desired response, try discussing the riveting issue of apostrophes.

The Cheltenham Festival, with its atmosphere of contentedness and hysteria, is on the 'must' list for horseracing bluffers, but do try to wheedle your way into someone's private box, or even get invited into one of the big bookmakers' boxes by losing a fortune to them. Wearing a clerical white collar sometimes helps, unless the box is reserved for atheists.

People look forward for months
to backing the wrong horse in the
Cheltenham Gold Cup.

As well as a terrific view of the racecourse's iconic amphitheatre (that's Cleeve Hill you're looking at), and a ham sandwich, it will give you somewhere to go for a bit of respite from the heaving masses, and a welcome sit-down, while you decide how you're going to win your money back.

AINTREE

In 1975, when Red Rum attempted a hat-trick of Grand National victories, just 9,000 people were there to watch him finish a gallant second to L'Escargot. Aintree, which had recently been bought by property developer Bill Davies, was teetering on the brink of closure.

A year later, Ladbrokes had taken over the course's management and a crowd of 42,000 saw Red Rum finish second again, this time to Rag Trade, before his memorable third victory in 1977.

In the early 1980s, the threat of closure loomed large once more and visitors to Aintree could easily see why. It was a run-down venue offering bleak facilities in a desolate location for a once-a-year tradition. There is still something bleak about the location but, now owned by Jockey Club Racecourses, the facilities are noticeably better and the three-day Grand National meeting offers a string of high-class races. In 2013, 28,000 attended on the Thursday, 45,000 on Friday and 66,000 on Saturday, when there was a peak television audience of almost 9 million. Yes, they're just numbers, but they point to one inescapable fact: The National is a race like no other, although a series of changes to its unique fences has made it a less formidable challenge than in Red Rum's day. Ladies Day at Aintree, on the Friday, offers another challenge, full of raucous parties, tight pink dresses, and heels that really weren't meant to walk on turf – unless to aerate it.

Make a point of walking round the National course before racing, and try to work out where the horse you back is going to fall. Then try walking round the Aintree Pavilion without treading on a discarded plastic glass. You may find that is a challenge too far.

YORK

Despite an outdated dress code, requiring men in the County Stand to display a stiff upper lip and stick it out in jackets and ties regardless of how hot it is, York is a friendly racecourse with fine facilities, a fine track and fine racing, all situated a pleasant walk away from the centre of a fine city when it's not periodically flooded by the River Ouse.

Meetings, particularly the John Smith's Cup and Music Showcase fixtures in July, attract justifiably large crowds, but the four-day Ebor Festival in August is the traditional highlight. The Ebor Handicap, over one and three-quarter miles, is the most valuable Flat handicap race in Europe and has been run at the Knavesmire since 1843. Three years later, the Gimcrack Stakes, named after a famous racehorse who won 27 of his 36 races between 1764 and 1771, was staged for the first time.

The race, for two-year-olds, is run over six furlongs. The bluffer might like to point out that Gimcrack never actually ran at York, didn't run as a two-year-old and never raced over six furlongs. The curiosity is explained by the fact that York-based admirers of the horse named their club, and subsequently a race, after Gimcrack. Traditionally, each December, the winning owner delivers a speech at the Gimcrack Club dinner. York racegoers clearly can't get enough Gimcrack. Nobody knows why.

The winning post at Bangor
is situated in a strange place, round
the corner from the spectators.
Perhaps it's so that they prolong the
delusion that their horse has won.

THE BEST OF THE REST

British racecourses are full of enjoyable idiosyncrasies and to get the best out of horseracing you need to sample the delights of smaller courses, many of them situated in the countryside.

Equine stars and high-profile races don't have to be on the menu for a thoroughly entertaining afternoon or evening, and the top jockeys regularly ride at smaller meetings.

There are too many racecourses to cover individually. Here is a potpourri of selected titbits about courses which the bluffer should be familiar with, followed by a bit about point-to-point racing – a very British idiosyncrasy.

BANGOR

It is important to go to the right one. Not Bangor on the Welsh coast opposite the island of Anglesey, where the University of Bangor and about 17,000 people live, but Bangor-Is-Y-Coed, alias Bangor-on-Dee, near Wrexham, where the racecourse and about 1,300 people live.

It's best when it's not raining, due to the absence of a grandstand. The winning post is situated in a strange place, round the corner from the spectators. Perhaps it's so that they prolong the delusion that their horse has won.

BATH

For the bluffer, the main thing to remember is that this was where one of the most famous acts of racing skulduggery took place.

— ♛ —

'Bath is the highest racecourse in Britain.'
Bath Racecourse

On 16 July 1953, Francasal won the Spa Selling Plate at a starting price of 10-1. The conspirators, led by one Harry Kateley, had staked the equivalent of £100,000 to win the equivalent of a present-day £1 million. They were confident Francasal would win because the horse was not Francasal but a better one, Santa Amaro. They were also confident that off-course bookmakers would not be able to phone bets to bookmakers at the racecourse, to shorten Francasal's odds, because they had cut the telephone lines.

Unfortunately for them, bookmakers resolutely refused to pay, the plot was exposed and four conspirators were sent to prison. When you go to Bath, it's always worth mentioning Francasal. Corruption in racing has become a lot more sophisticated since then, you might observe shaking your head sadly.

BRIGHTON

The place to start is at the pitch-and-putt course on the seafront near Roedean School for girls. There's a cafe there where you can carry out a post-mortem on your golf and study the form before heading up the hill to the racecourse.

When you arrive, there are several worthwhile views, although the undistinguished blocks of flats on the far side of the track are not among them. There's a view of the sea or, possibly, of a sea fret (a thick fog which rolls in without warning). There's also a view of the extraordinary helter-skelter downhill track and, on the staircase up to Silks Restaurant, there are some lovely black-and-white photographs from the days when the crowds were a lot bigger and no blocks of flats blighted the landscape.

CARTMEL

On the edge of the Lake District and tremendously popular, the racecourse boasts a sign advising visitors that, from June to August 'The water irrigation system will be in use. Members of the general public may get wet.'

Owned by Lord Cavendish of Furness, who lives in nearby Holker Hall, Cartmel has several unique features, among them a curiously arranged track, an interesting array of stalls, including displays of owls and eagles and, in the local village shop, Cartmel's world famous sticky toffee pudding. Excellent.

CHESTER

An intimate racecourse popularly known as the 'Roodee', where the tight, one-mile-around track gives racegoers – and there tend to be a lot of them – a feeling of involvement. There's a party atmosphere. Jeffrey Bernard, the racing journalist and *The Spectator* magazine columnist who was the subject of the play *Jeffrey Bernard is Unwell,* wrote, 'When I die, I'd like to be buried at Chester, if there's room.' His wish was unfulfilled, like many of his bets, which were doubtless the victims of either a poor draw or a slow start, much like everyone else's bets.

The bluffer will be able to remind companions that racing has been staged at the Roodee since 1539. As evidence, a plaque on the city wall above the racecourse states, 'Horse racing in Chester began in 1539 after football was banned because so many players got hurt.'

EXETER

A splendid country jumps course not only near Exeter but also not far from The Nobody Inn at Doddiscombsleigh,

♛

Exeter is the highest racecourse in the land.

Exeter Racecourse

which might be a rare opportunity to have a drink in a pun (something to do with a former landlord failing in his wish to hold his funeral wake there). While Chester is one mile around, Exeter is two miles around and popular with countrymen taking a day off from killing things.

Best Mate, who later won the Cheltenham Gold Cup three times in a row (2002 to 2004) made his first appearance over fences at Exeter. A lot of people already know that, so it might be better to focus on the splendid Nobody Inn. It's a strange one, but well worth visiting – if you can find it.

FAKENHAM

It helps if you like long drives and seafood. When you finally arrive (it's in north Norfolk), the effort's worth it. The anticlockwise track is rather like Chester but with jumps, and suits horses whose left legs are shorter than their right ones. It suited Prince Carlton, who won there 10 times, on the last occasion when he was aged 15, in 1990. You may have to tell people that, because they're unlikely to tell you.

FONTWELL

Several things for bluffers to note. First, Fontwell is the only jumps course with a figure-of-eight track. Second, it was the scene of the Queen's first winner as an owner. The horse was Monaveen and the date 10 October 1949, when the Queen wasn't the Queen but was still Princess Elizabeth. Third, Fontwell is four miles from Arundel Castle, the home of the successive Dukes of Norfolk.

You are unlikely to see the current 18th Duke of Norfolk at Fontwell because he is more interested in the Scout movement than horseracing, unlike the 16th Duke who was the Queen's representative at Ascot and, in 1971, stepped in to ban hot pants. Spoilsport.

HEXHAM

Near Hadrian's Wall, which fails to keep out the wind. The course's main attribute is its lovely view of the Northumberland countryside. Largely owned by Charles Enderby, member of the Queen's bodyguard and former

Hexham racecourse is the highest National Hunt course in the UK.

Hexham Racecourse

High Sheriff of Northumberland, Hexham boasts the steepest parade ring in Britain. Its best known race is the intriguingly named Heart Of All England Maiden Hunters' Chase. A friendly, jumping enthusiasts' course, with a racecard that once featured the memorable line, 'We apologise for our main building clock being out of action. Clock repairer coming when he has time.'

KELSO

Racecourses owned by the aristocracy are invariably idiosyncratic. The 10th Duke of Roxburghe owns the land which a higgledy-piggledy assortment of buildings occupy, including the main stand, built in 1822. This can be regarded either as a listed architectural treasure or (more accurately) as a bit of a mess featuring various unfortunate accretions.

A welcoming racecourse in the Scottish Borders, Kelso rises above its defects and if you look towards the Cheviot Hills, you will see an obelisk built in honour of one James Thomson, who wrote the words to 'Rule, Britannia!' If you back a winner, you might feel an urge to sing them.

LUDLOW

Another fiefdom of the landed aristocracy, this time represented by the Earl of Plymouth Estates. There are various inconveniences, including seven road crossings, the need to cross the track to get to the parade ring and a railway behind the grandstand which doesn't offer stopping trains but acts as a barrier to expansion. However, there is one considerable convenience – a set of Edwardian urinals made by Scull Bros of Shrewsbury.

MARKET RASEN

A very pleasant and well-managed country jumps course with some attractive and popular meetings. You may want to use the David Ashforth Toilets, a source of pride, at least to the author.

PERTH

A lively, friendly place much loved by distant trainers such as Gordon Elliott (from Ireland) and Nigel Twiston-Davies (from England). The Nelson Stand is not, a bluffer might knowledgeably point out, named after Admiral Nelson, who did not contribute to the stand's erection, but after an entirely different Nelson who did.

If you walk to the far side of the track, you will be able to inspect the silvery River Tay (much beloved by the world's worst poet William McGonagall*), as well as the two-mile start. If you walk off the racecourse altogether, you may find the Earl of Mansfield in nearby Scone Palace.

PLUMPTON

Another country jumps track that provokes fondness in its patrons. A compact track (easy viewing) with compact facilities (no long walks required). Built on clay, when it rained the going used to be very heavy but, since they discovered drainage, heavy going is confined largely to the betting ring.

There are some good pubs in the area but you'll have to discover them for yourself. A good bluffer won't remember what they are called.

SALISBURY

An absolutely splendid course. A lovely setting, it's always sunny and there are swallows (or is it swifts, or house martins?) in the grandstand, wondering what on earth's going on. Eyesight permitting, you can see Salisbury Cathedral in the distance and, all in all, all's well with the world.

A bluffer might care to let it be known that the cathedral

---

* See *The Bluffer's Guide to Poetry*.

houses a copy of the Magna Carta and that the late prime minister Edward Heath lived in Cathedral Close. He wasn't a racing man. He liked boats. More fool him.

'Folkestone is very possibly the lowest racecourse in the UK. Or might be if it hadn't closed.'

Bluffer's Media

TOWCESTER

As curious as its owner, Lord Hesketh, the racecourse offers the rare experience of free admission to most meetings. There used to be a lovely view of the Northamptonshire countryside before they built a greyhound track on it. The part preserved for horses goes a long way downhill, with the result that it is a long way uphill to the finishing line. For a small course, it has some rather fine buildings. The Empress Stand, in a sort of Chinese art deco style, is named after the Empress of Austria, who was killed by an anarchist in 1898, should anyone ask. You're probably safe; the anarchist died some time ago.

WINDSOR

A humbler version of Goodwood but nearer the River Thames, the Royal Windsor Racecourse is best known for its Monday evening meetings, which are recommended. There's a boat service from The Promenade in Windsor and a nice atmosphere helped along by a younger-than-usual crowd.

Robert Morley, the endearing actor and racehorse owner, was a regular visitor, even when he wasn't young. Allegedly, he once encouraged the film director John Huston to bid for the winner of a selling race. A short while later the horse fell down dead. Hopefully you'll be luckier.

POINT-TO-POINT RACING

From December to June, the hunting fraternity stage race meetings at over 100 point-to-point courses. The races are all chases, mainly over three miles, with amateur riders on board horses that have qualified by being taken hunting. Many of the horses are ex-racehorses and the better point-to-pointers compete in hunter chase races at 'normal' race meetings.

The meetings often attract big crowds, despite being held at venues which Victorian explorers would have struggled to find. They have intriguing names, such as the Duke of Buccleuch's at Friars Haugh, the Black Forest Club at Black Forest Lodge, possibly in Germany, the Dulverton Farmers at Treborough Hill, and the charming Derwent at Charm Park.

If you manage to find one, expect a lot of SUVs, hampers, tweed clothing and shooting sticks, in case anything worth shooting flies past. All in all, it's good fun.

AND THEY'RE OFF!

I t takes all sorts to make a race crowd. In the old days the classes were segregated into different enclosures: upper classes in the Members' enclosure with ready access to the best facilities, parade ring and sight of the winning post; working classes in the Silver Ring or beyond, with ready access to the worst facilities, remote from both the parade ring and winning post. There is as yet no Bluffer's enclosure, but perhaps there should be.

Society has changed and racecourses have changed with it. Today, segregation is based largely on money – money and badges. Temporary cash flow difficulties may make the bluffer wince at the price of admission to, say, the Club Enclosure at Cheltenham on Gold Cup Day (£90). On the other hand, he may not be content with admission to a twilight meeting on the all-weather track at Kempton Park (£12) nor a meeting at Towcester (£0). The answer is a badge.

A racehorse owner with a horse running that day is entitled to a number of admission badges, as are sponsors of the races. The bluffer may not be an owner or sponsor himself, but it behoves him to know someone who is, and befriend him or her. Everybody likes to have friends, especially if they have badges.

The right badge is a passport, not only to the right enclosure but also to the delights of the owners and trainers bar, and the sponsors' boxes. Any box is better than no box at all. Bluffer, badge and box are made for each other.

If the bluffer cannot bluff his way in, he could try climbing in, taking care not to rip his trousers while trying to avoid being escorted unceremoniously from the premises, possibly by the police.

ESSENTIAL EQUIPMENT

As a racing man (or woman), the bluffer will be accompanied by a copy of the *Racing Post*, a sign that he takes the subject seriously.

Binoculars, once de rigueur, have been rendered largely redundant by the arrival of big screens – very big ones – much bigger than the one in your living room. It is still advisable to take binoculars. Big screens are not always available; binoculars suggest a racegoer of standing, if also of some vintage, and there is always the chance of spotting a rare bird, a dodo perhaps.

The addition of a racecard makes a total of three items, compared to your two hands. Pockets (racecard) and shoulders (binoculars) are a help but an umbrella is a hindrance. If you bring it, you'll only lose it. Better to leave the umbrella in the car, then be resolutely uncomplaining when it pours with rain, especially if you've forgotten your raincoat.

WHAT TO WEAR

This depends largely on whether you are a man or a woman, and which racecourse you are visiting, on which day. If Grayson Perry chose to wear the same outfit he wore when receiving the CBE from Prince Charles, a midnight blue dress and jacket, with a black hat, it would not go unnoticed on a Wednesday afternoon at Redcar but would fit in nicely on Ladies Day at Royal Ascot.

Racecourses have dress codes of varying degrees of rigour. At York, 'Gentlemen are required to wear a jacket, collared shirt and tie in the County Stand' while 'Ladies are required to dress in a suitable manner. Imagine you are going to a smart wedding is our tip.'

Cheltenham, however, does not have a dress code and 'Fancy dress is permitted.' Many racegoers interpret this as an encouragement to wear tweeds. At Aintree, there is 'no strict dress code but smart dress is preferable,' guidance popularly translated into tight pink dresses and vertiginous heels, with the occasional Elvis Presley impersonator thrown in.

The bluffer will, no doubt, have a fine collection of fake designer clothes and accessories to choose from. Generally, dress is less formal at jumps meetings (cold and wet) than at Flat fixtures (warm and dry), except at summer jumps meetings (warm and dry) and winter Flat fixtures (cold and wet).

Curiously, the more you pay to go in, the less choice you are allowed when deciding what to wear. Those in the cheapest enclosure tend to be regarded as beyond sartorial hope and are prone to appear wearing shorts, T-shirts, rings, possibly through their nose, and tattoos.

If you are thinking of walking the course before racing (you probably aren't), wellington boots are advisable, as are enquiries as to the circumference of the track. If, while walking the course, you encounter a man prodding a stick into the ground, he is probably the clerk of the course. His job is to walk round and, on returning to his office, announce that the going is 'good to soft', which is what he, and most trainers, hoped it would be.

EATING AND DRINKING

Racecourse food used to be terrible and the best advice was to ask for the sweetie stall and find comfort in a bar of chocolate full of those E-numbers. It's a lot better now and racecourse restaurants are virtually unrecognisable from their predecessors.

Chester's 1539 restaurant currently provides the chance to launch yourself into the Johnson and Swarbrick confit duck and coriander cress, duo of carrot and soy, before moving on to the main dish, perhaps of roast chump of Conwy Valley lamb, gnocchi, butternut squash, rosemary juices and ricotta, before rounding off with Bramley apple and fig crumble, cinnamon mascarpone. Nothing too pretentious.

At the top end, it's expensive. If you fancy lunch and tea in the Double Trigger Restaurant during Glorious Goodwood, it will cost at least £124 per person, but only if you are a member. If you're not, you're ineligible and may have to resort to the Sussex Bistro, where lunch costs only £72.

If you prefer a burger or fish and chips, you are unlikely to have trouble finding them, although finding somewhere to sit down to eat them is often more of a challenge. Racecourses tend to be good at the top end, good at the fast-food end, but less good in the middle.

♛

'Lunatics; horse-mad, betting-mad, drunken-mad, vice-mad.'

Charles Dickens meets a race crowd at Doncaster in 1857

There are plenty of bars and, at some meetings at some courses, too many over-enthusiastic drinkers. On the whole, though, the atmosphere at racecourses is one of the sport's most attractive features. People want to be there and are in a good mood, at least until the favourite falls at the last fence. Their mood is improved by the thought that they aren't either a) at work or b) at home cleaning the bath. Smiles are commonplace, even though the sun will burn up in about 5 billion years time, and where will we be then?

TALKING THE TALK

Social anthropologist Kate Fox, in her entertaining book *The Racing Tribe* (1999), identified an appealing 'social micro-climate' at racecourses. In this 'alternative reality', social rules and restrictions are relaxed, making it permissible and normal for complete strangers to interact more readily than elsewhere. The intervals between races provide good opportunities to do so and there is a lot of eye contact, smiling and conversation, as well as drinking.

Even a socially unaccomplished bluffer will find it easy to engage in conversation, for the horses and races, as well as fellow racegoers, provide ready subjects for discussion. Many a relationship has been launched with the unpromising opening, 'What do you fancy?' or 'Did you back that winner?'

The bar, the viewing areas, the parade ring and the railings surrounding the winner's enclosure are all venues for socialising, and for a display of knowledge or, at least, opinions.

Before each race, the bluffer will be inclined to study the horses with a relaxed yet intent eye as they are led around the parade ring. 'He looks well,' is a pretty safe comment unless, of course, it's a she. Good signs are an enthusiastic but not frenetic walk, a bright eye, alert ears, shiny coat and good muscle tone. Bad signs are heavy sweating and erections.

When they canter to the start, good signs are horses that are relaxed, settled and move comfortably and easily. Bad signs are horses that refuse to go to the start or gallop off uncontrollably, pausing for breath only after unseating their rider and completing a circuit of the track – two circuits if it's Chester.

There is plenty of scope for discussing a horse's chance of success before the race, and for pondering the reason for its failure afterwards. As in many walks of life, the merit of an opinion is commonly, if erroneously, regarded more highly when delivered with confidence. For example, the bluffer will know to express the view 'He gave the favourite a poor ride,' in a tone that brooks no argument, and alerts listeners to the likelihood of finding themselves in one should they challenge it. It cannot be overemphasised that all opinions of this sort should be assertively expressed. And, of course, there are plenty more where they came from – the bluffer's imagination.

WATCHING A RACE

Like life, every race has a start, a middle and an end. Also like life, all can be disastrous.

On the Flat, virtually all races use starting stalls in a determined but still sometimes failed attempt to get the horses off on level terms. Having been driven 200 miles to the racecourse, a horse sometimes refuses to go into the stalls although he is perfectly happy to be driven 200 miles back home for dinner.

It is not unknown for the stalls to open and an occupant to stand perfectly still, as content and untroubled as his rider is the opposite. In a famous 1980s advertisement for Hamlet cigars, a horse stays in the stalls while Jacques Loussier plays Bach's 'Air on the G String' and the resigned jockey lights up a cigar. 'Happiness is a cigar called Hamlet.' Or was until advertisements for cigars were banned.

More commonly, a horse emerges, slowly, resulting in an analyst's final comment, 'Started slowly, faded.'

At some tracks, over certain distances, the horse's draw – the stall it is allocated – can be very important. Stalls are numbered from the inside running rail, so the horse drawn nearest to the rail is in stall 1. At Chester and Beverley, for instance, particularly in sprints, over five or six furlongs, a low draw bestows a significant advantage. Horses drawn badly have a tendency to fall sick and be withdrawn with a vet's certificate. If they run, it is part of a jockey's expertise to exploit a good draw or overcome a bad one.

Reading a race, interpreting what is going on, is a skill that takes a while to acquire. At a higher level, it involves knowing the characteristics of individual horses – whether or not they are likely to be suited by the distance of the race, by a fast-run race, by the conformation of the track and the state of the going. Some horses perform best when making the running, preferably without being harassed by another horse, while others, particularly those with a 'turn of foot', the ability to accelerate, are more likely to be 'held up' and brought with a 'late run'.

Jockeys prepare for a race by trying to work out how it is likely to unfold. Which horses are likely to make the running? What is the pace likely to be? What tactics should the jockey adopt, or attempt, to maximise his chance of success?

The bluffer's race-reading skills may be unsophisticated and his attention focused on the single horse that he has a particular interest in, and perhaps has backed. Even so, there are certain things that are worth observing. What you are hoping to see is the horse travelling well, preferably in the right direction, and positioned to provide every opportunity of winning. In a jump race, you also want to see it jumping well and economically.

You don't want to see a horse racing too keenly and failing to settle, which will expend energy and take its toll later on. If the pace is slow, you do not want the horse to be held up a long way 'off the pace'. At some point the pace will quicken and the horse is likely to struggle to make up the deficit.

By watching races you can learn how to 'read' a race, which gives more meaning and enjoyment to the sport. And at the same time makes your utterings more credible.

'Nothing matters more to a trainer than winning the Derby.'

Sir Michael Stoute, trainer of five Derby winners

GREAT RACES

In the public mind, two British races reign supreme, the Derby and the Grand National. People who rarely watch racing or bet will do both for those two races, particularly the Grand National, seen as a bit of a lottery offering the chance of a long-priced winner picked with a pin.

Both races have long and chequered histories, and both have changed a lot in recent times. The Derby, which once saw Parliament closed for the day and London society, high and low, make its way to Epsom Downs, was moved from its traditional Wednesday to Saturday in 1995 in an attempt to reverse the Derby's declining popularity. That, and other initiatives, irritated traditionalists but resulted in bigger crowds – an estimated 120,000 in 2013, most of them on the Hill in the centre of the course, where pedestrians are entitled to free entry.

Aintree has experienced even more dramatic fluctuations in fortune, with the Grand National facing threats to its future on several occasions, but now attracting big crowds to a much improved racecourse. Equine welfare concerns have prompted a series of changes which have made the formidable National course less formidable and the outcome of the race, at least in theory, less unpredictable.

The bluffer is already well aware of all this, but a few reminders never go amiss.

THE DERBY

It can seem to take a long time to get to Epsom and, when you've arrived, there are two ways of judging the course. It's either a very silly track on which to stage a race as important as the Derby, or it's the perfect test of a thoroughbred racehorse, especially one with ambitions to sire other racehorses.

Both jockeys and horses have to think quite hard, and quickly, because if they're not going uphill or downhill (Tattenham Hill), they're rounding a bend (Tattenham Corner) and, as they gallop down the home straight, they have to deal with a camber that tries to roll them towards the far rail. Success requires balance, speed, stamina and heart. Punters require tolerance and resilience. And a lot of luck.

There are plenty of names from the past to toy with, both famous and infamous. Running Rein, the winner of the 1844 Derby, was particularly unusual because he was actually another horse, Maccabeus. The Derby is restricted to three-year-olds and Maccabeus was a four-year-old, which gave him a significant advantage. Unfortunately for Goodman Levy, the bookmaker behind the deception, the fraud was exposed, the winner disqualified and the runner-up, Orlando, declared the victor.

Some great horses have won the Derby but none have been greater than Sea-Bird, the 1965 winner, who laughed contemptuously (if metaphorically) at his opponents, and went on to laugh again at a distinguished collection of rivals in the Prix de l'Arc de Triomphe, at Longchamp. Sea-Bird was a bit like Arkle, but jumped fewer fences and had a shorter career, embracing just eight races.

Then there was Nijinsky, who won the Triple Crown, a rarely attempted hat-trick made up of the 2000 Guineas, the Derby and the St Leger, the first over one mile, the second over one and a half miles, and the third over one and three quarter miles. They are three of the five English Classics, all confined to three-year-olds. The other two are the 1000 Guineas and Oaks, both restricted to fillies.

Nijinsky's triumph was in 1970. A year later, another exceptional horse, Mill Reef, won the Derby. Mill Reef wasn't just extremely good, he was also exceptionally versatile and tough. It is very rare for a horse that is outstanding over sprint distances as a two-year-old to be equally good as a three-year-old, over much longer distances. Mill Reef was, winning the six-furlong Coventry Stakes and Gimcrack Stakes in 1970, as well as the seven-furlong Dewhurst Stakes, then, in 1971, winning the Eclipse Stakes over a mile and a quarter and the King George VI and Queen Elizabeth Stakes and Prix de l'Arc de Triomphe, both over a mile and a half. You might need to come back to this.

That year, there happened to be another outstanding

three-year-old, Brigadier Gerard. On the only occasion the two met, in the 2000 Guineas, Brigadier Gerard was the winner, but that was over one mile, his best distance but short of Mill Reef's best. It meant that the argument over which was the best rolled on without conclusion, although with progressively fewer of those who saw the two equine giants in live action still alive to argue about it. In time, the debate will become entirely posthumous, so there's no need to worry about it too much.

♛

'Why all the fuss? After all,
the Derby is just another race.'

*Lester Piggott after winning his first Derby on
Never Say Die in 1954*

Mill Reef went on to sire two Derby winners, Shirley Heights (1978) and Reference Point (1987). Shergar, who won the 1981 Derby by a record 10 lengths, had little opportunity to do the same. In 1983 he was kidnapped from the Ballymany Stud in Ireland, by the IRA, and subsequently killed.

The roll of honour rolls on, taking in Nashwan (1989), Generous (1991), Lammtarra (1995), Galileo (2001) and Sea The Stars (2009). The bluffer may want to move beyond the mere commonplace recital of Derby winners to the recital of Derby losers, with particular reference to Dancing Brave.

'Has there ever been a more unlucky loser than Dancing Brave?' would be a fruitful opening line. The obvious, and correct, answer is, 'Who knows? The Derby's been going since 1780 and I missed a lot of the early ones,' but the bluffer should not be deterred by that minor inconvenience. Better to plough on with, 'I don't think so. What a terrible ride Greville Starkey gave Dancing Brave, didn't he?' Then stand back.

It was 1986 and Dancing Brave was a superstar. That year he won the 2000 Guineas, Eclipse Stakes, King George VI and Queen Elizabeth Stakes and Prix de l'Arc de Triomphe. He would have won the Derby but Starkey got too far behind, set his mount an impossible task and Dancing Brave couldn't quite catch Shahrastani.

Great horses and great riders tend to go together. Lester Piggott was known as 'the housewives' favourite', not because of excessive charm – he was generally monosyllabic and taciturn and nicknamed 'Old Stoneface' – but because whatever he rode in the Derby had a habit of winning. Piggott won the Derby nine times, starting with Never Say Die in 1954, when Piggott was only 18, and finishing with Teenoso in 1983 when he was 47.

One of the best Derby-winning riders was Steve Cauthen, another precocious talent who, aged 18, won the 1978 US Triple Crown (the Kentucky Derby, Preakness Stakes and Belmont Stakes) on Affirmed. Cauthen moved to Britain and won the Derby on Slip Anchor in 1985 and on Reference Point two years later, on both occasions leading all the way. The Derby is a searching test of a jockey's skill and judgement of pace, and Cauthen had plenty of both.

Nowadays, you won't see either Piggott (retired and old) or Cauthen (retired and less old) riding in the Derby, but you will see the Queen's Stand (she didn't build it herself), opened in 1992, and the Hill in the centre of the course. They are very different.

To gain admittance to the Queen's Stand, you will need to wear morning dress with a top hat, unless you are a woman, in which case you will need to wear a formal dress or a tailored trouser suit. On the Hill, there are no such restrictions. Many men favour shorts, sandals, a T-shirt and tattoos, while many women favour tight blouses.

If you have a baby you would like to exchange, this is the place to go, for there are an enormous number of babies in prams, and quite a lot of young ladies who look as if they will be in need of a pram soon.

There are also fairground rides and market stalls selling a huge range of goods of dubious provenance. And, of course, there is Betsy Lee, and various related fortune tellers, operating from caravans that have seen better days. Outside are boards recording famous clients of the past, most of them long dead. Perhaps Betsy Lee forecast their demise.

THE GRAND NATIONAL

The most famous horse race in the world, and the only one that has fences with names that people recognise – Becher's Brook, the Chair, the Canal Turn, Valentine's Brook.

Large fences tend to cause horses to fall over, sometimes with fatal consequences. For a long time, this didn't seem to bother people unduly, but more recently it has and, as a result, the Grand National fences have been made progressively easier.

♛

'The Grand National is simply the world's greatest steeplechase.'

Jonjo O'Neill, Grand National winning trainer and former champion jump jockey

---

Some enthusiasts, particularly those aged over 60, regard this as a sad state of affairs and hanker for the days when the Grand National brought back happy memories of the Charge of the Light Brigade, but with fewer guns. Other enthusiasts, particularly those aged under 40, regard the changes as a jolly good thing and quite right too. This is something the bluffer ought to have an opinion about. It doesn't matter greatly what your opinion is, as long as you've got one and are prepared to argue for it, fiercely. The bluffer can be as passionate as the next fanatic.

Gone, sadly, or happily, are the prospects of another 1967, when there was an enormous pile-up at the 23rd fence, caused by a loose horse. Foinavon, at 100-1, was so far behind that John Buckingham, his jockey, had time to find a careful passage through the melee, emerging in splendid isolation to plod on to glory, to the delight of the bookmaking industry. The fence is now known as Foinavon.

The humblest race fan will have a stock of Grand National knowledge and names at his or her disposal and the bluffer should listen in neutral mode to the annual recital of the achievements of Red Rum and of the epic 1973 battle between trainer Ginger McCain's hero and the mighty Crisp. There will be talk of the brave and eccentric Duke of Albuquerque, who never won the National but broke a lot of bones trying to, and of the brave Bob Champion, who returned from cancer to win the National in 1981, on Aldaniti. All this the bluffer will allow to float by before interjecting, 'Does anyone know which jockey has won most Grand Nationals?'

A short silence can be expected, followed by a few unsuccessful stabs in the dark. This is the time for you to allow yourself a slightly smug, condescending smirk, interspersed with, 'No, no, it wasn't him. No, nor him. I'm surprised no one knows. Does anyone follow racing?' Then, with a resigned sigh, 'Well, I suppose I'll have to tell you. It was, of course, George Stevens. He won five times between 1856 and 1870. First there was Freetrader, then two sisters, Emblem and Emblematic, in 1863 and 1864, and then The Colonel. Amazingly, he was having only his second race over fences when he won in 1869, and didn't race again until winning the next year. Poor George. He was killed in a riding accident a few months later."

Yes, that should work.

PATTERN AND LISTED RACES

At the narrow top of the pyramid of races are a select group of Pattern races. On the Flat, they are divided into Groups 1, 2 and 3.

In 2014, the Derby was one of just 33 Group 1 races, with Ascot and Newmarket staging 20 of them. There were 45 Group 2 races and 68 Group 3 races. Below the Pattern races were 143 Listed races.

Over jumps, there is a similar system. During the 2014/15 season, there were 39 Grade 1 races, 24 of them at either Cheltenham or Aintree. There were 60 Grade 2 races and 37 Grade 3 races, with 65 Listed races below them.

The bluffer may well choose to pose a particular question. That question is, 'What Grade race is the Grand National?' The rather surprising answer (hence the bluffer's question) is 'Grade 3'. The National is by far the most valuable jump race, offering prize money totalling £1 million, but it is a handicap (*see* next chapter) and, neither over jumps nor on the Flat, are any handicaps awarded Grade 1 or Group 1 status.

'The job of the handicapper is to provide a puzzle which it is difficult for the public to solve.'

Phil Smith, British Horseracing Authority's Head of Handicapping

HANDICAPS
AND OTHER HURDLES

Well over half of all the horse races in Britain are handicaps, with horses carrying different weights based on the official handicapper's assessment of their past performances. It is a way of bringing horses of different abilities together or, put another way, of making it jolly difficult to work out which one will win.

The handicapper's job appeals to certain types of people. Albert Pierrepoint, for instance, who killed over 400 men and women with the government's approval, might have made a fine handicapper had he not opted for life as a hangman. Like Pierrepoint, handicappers are always upsetting people.

In a handicap race, it is not enough to work out which horse is the best (in theory, the one allotted the highest weight), you have to work out which one is 'best handicapped'. Is there a horse which you believe has a handicap rating that understates its likely level of performance in the race in question?

Perhaps today's conditions – the state of the ground, the distance of the race, the conformation of the racecourse, the speed at which the race is likely to be run, the rider on board – will enable the horse, perhaps an improving one, to perform better than in its recent races. That sort of thing.

Fortunately for the bluffer, some handy expressions are at hand. 'He looks well handicapped to me,' is common currency, as is 'He doesn't look very well handicapped to me.' Either can be applied in a wide range of cases, as can 'I've got a feeling he may be better than his rating,' or 'I'm not sure he's worth his rating.'

Since opinions differ so much, almost any of those will do although, when talking to a trainer, it is best to suggest that the handicapper has treated his horse harshly rather than leniently. This gives the trainer an opportunity, likely to be seized with relish, to rail against the unreasonable nature of handicappers in general, with particular reference to their vindictive treatment of horses trained by himself. Nods of agreement by the bluffer are certain to meet with approval.

Since a horse's handicap mark influences its prospects of winning, trainers are sometimes tempted to take steps to influence its rating, some of the steps being within the rules of racing, others outside them.

In 1849, Admiral Henry Rous, a hugely influential figure in the sport, declared, 'Every great handicap offers a premium to fraud.' Over 150 years later, Mark Johnston, a leading trainer, complained that racing's rulers spent enormous amounts of time and money trying to ensure the integrity of horseracing 'while operating a handicap system which encourages and often rewards cheating.'

There have always been trainers and jockeys who try to conceal a horse's real ability by deliberately not trying to win a race, with the aim of persuading the handicapper to reduce the horse's handicap mark, thereby making it 'well handicapped'. That is a serious breach of the rules, liable to result in a severe penalty, if proven.

Improvements in technology, access to betting data and standards of stewarding have made it easier to detect 'non-triers' although, like the poor, they are always with us.

There are other, less crude methods of getting a horse well handicapped, such as running it over unsuitable distances or on unfavourable going. For punters, this is either a fascinating aspect of the crossword puzzle or a tremendous irritation provoking moral outrage.

NON-HANDICAP RACES

In these races, the weight each horse carries is determined by the published conditions of the race. Horses contesting races confined to horses of the same age often carry the same weight, with a weight allowance for fillies and mares racing against colts and geldings. Previous winners may have to carry a weight penalty which may vary according to the number and nature of the race or races previously won.

Where horses of different ages contest the same race, the weights they carry are based on the 'weight-for-age scale', a refined version of a system invented by Admiral Rous in 1850 and revised by him in 1873. It makes allowance for the relative maturity of horses of different ages so that, depending on the time of year and distance of the race, a three-year-old will carry less weight than a four-year-old or older horse. Simple really.

SUB-GENRES

Within the broad categories of handicap and non-handicap races are all sorts of sub-divisions, and all sorts of race distances. On the Flat, the shortest distance is five furlongs and the longest, the Queen Alexandra Stakes at Royal Ascot, almost two and three-quarter miles. Over jumps, the shortest distance in both hurdle races and chases (*see* page 71) is two miles. The longest hurdle race is almost three and a half miles and the longest chase, the Grand National, almost four and a half miles.

OTHER SUB-DIVISIONS INCLUDE:

Amateur riders races Races for jockeys prepared to risk killing themselves without being paid for it.

Apprentice races An apprentice jockey is like an apprentice electrician, and similarly dangerous. Races confined to apprentices offer the sight of a small, inexperienced mammal sitting on a much larger one, travelling at over 30 mph.

Bumper races The popular name for National Hunt Flat races. These are for horses not quick enough to race on the Flat but unable to jump properly yet.

Claiming races Horses are entered to be claimed for a range of prices, with the claiming price determining the weight the horse carries. By choosing a low claiming price, the trainer can improve the horse's chance of winning because it will carry a lower weight. For good or ill, it will also increase the likelihood of other people claiming the horse.

Hurdle races Races supplied with obstacles to increase the chance that the one you have backed falls over.

Juvenile races Races for delinquents. On the Flat, two-year-olds are regarded as juveniles. Over hurdles, juvenile races are for three-year-olds from October to December and for four-year-olds from January to April.

Maiden races Races for horses that have not yet won one, and are unlikely to.

Selling race Races in which the winner is offered for sale at a post-race auction, bidding to start at a sum specified in the race conditions. The current owner can bid for his own horse, thereby providing the opportunity to win the race yet lose money.

Steeplechases Races supplied with obstacles larger than hurdles for horses that have failed to fall over in hurdle races.

Whatever the type of race, most races are for moderate horses because that is what most racehorses are. Owners and trainers dream of winning races at Royal Ascot or the Cheltenham Festival but the reality is that, if they win a race at all, it is far more likely to be at Lingfield or Ludlow.

Luckily, there is a lot of fun to be had with horses that are what school teachers long ago used to refer to as 'duffers'. The trick is to find a race populated by other, even more complete duffers.

There are plenty of races where it is difficult to imagine any of the participants winning but – one of the beauties of horseracing – one has to win. Granted, the prize money may be paltry as may the number of racegoers present to appreciate and applaud the winner, but think of the

♛

> There are plenty of races where it is difficult to imagine any of the participants winning.

thousands of people watching at home or in a betting shop. Imagine that the winning horse is The Bluffer. Thousands of race fans (well, punters, anyway) will share the owner's, trainer's and jockey's delight at The Bluffer's success. Obviously, many more thousands who backed the runner-up will be less appreciative. Tough.

RUNNERS...

Other sports have their human heroes but only horseracing has its equine heroes. Arkle and Desert Orchid, Lammtarra and Frankel are part of the enthusiast's vocabulary. Enthusiasts have read the racing dictionary from beginning to end, several times. The bluffer has not. You barely know where the dictionary is. When you find it, the trick is to pick out a few good words and bring them tellingly into the conversation.

So it is not the bluffer's job to retell the oft-told tale of Arkle, which is just as well, because you don't know what it is. While others will assume that you know the essentials, it is your pleasure to point to less familiar elements of the story – some conversational titbits. It's time to bluff that you know more than you do.

GREAT HORSES – A SAMPLE

ARKLE

(Cheltenham Gold Cup 1964, 1965, 1966. Irish Grand National 1964. Hennessy Gold Cup 1964, 1965. Whitbread

Gold Cup 1965. King George VI Chase 1965, plus 19 other wins.)

'Did you know that Anne, Duchess of Westminster, always used a cigarette holder when smoking? She used one when I visited her at Eaton Lodge. A beautiful spot, in Cheshire, have you been? No!

'As you know, the Duchess didn't just own Arkle. His three Gold Cups were on a table in the dining room, as was the one won by Ten Up in 1975. The trophy for Last Suspect's Grand National win in 1985 was there, too. We used to have salmon for lunch, from her Scottish estate. A lovely lady. Happy memories.'

DESERT ORCHID

(Cheltenham Gold Cup 1989. King George VI Chase 1986, 1988, 1989, 1990. Whitbread Gold Cup 1988. Tingle Creek Chase 1988. Racing Post Chase 1990. Irish Grand National 1990, plus 25 other wins.)

'That day in 1989 when he won the Cheltenham Gold Cup was wonderful. Has it ever been so muddy? Of course, there was no drainage worth the name in those days. It was marvellous how Dessie battled but, for me, his Whitbread Gold Cup win the previous year was just as thrilling. I don't know about you but I didn't think he'd stay the trip. Three miles, five and a half furlongs! What did you think?'

ECLIPSE

(Five King's Plates 1769, six King's Plates 1770, plus seven other wins.)

'What people forget, of course, is that although Eclipse was unbeaten in 18 races, eight of them were walkovers and he never faced more than four opponents. He only beat 20 horses altogether. Obviously, he was a great sire but his owner was more interesting.

♛

Eclipse first and the rest nowhere.

Dennis O'Kelly, owner of Eclipse

'That was Dennis O'Kelly, an Irish rascal who met Charlotte Hayes, a prostitute, in the Fleet debtor's prison and set up in business with her. He conned gentlemen out of their money and she got them to spend more in her brothel. It paid for the racehorses, and for property. They did very well but the Jockey Club never would admit O'Kelly as a member.

'His skeleton's at North Mymms. Eclipse's, not O'Kelly's. It's in the Eclipse Building at the Royal Veterinary College. His heart weighed 14lb, you know. Eclipse's, not O'Kelly's. I don't know how much O'Kelly's weighed. He was probably heartless.'

FRANKEL

(Dewhurst Stakes 2010. 2000 Guineas, St James's Palace Stakes, Sussex Stakes, Queen Elizabeth II Stakes 2011. Lockinge Stakes, Queen Anne Stakes, Sussex Stakes,

Juddmonte International, Champion Stakes 2012, plus four other wins.)

Frankel, unbeaten in 14 races, trained by the ailing, much loved Sir Henry Cecil and ridden by jockey Tom Queally, was hailed as the greatest racehorse of modern times. Everybody knows that and you will not waste time repeating it – it's old hat. Instead, the bluffer might say, 'What people forget is how great a sadness it was to Prince Khalid Abdullah that Bobby Frankel didn't live to see Frankel race.

'As you know, Frankel trained the Prince's horses in the USA and the horse was named after him. Like Cecil, Frankel was a sick man. He died of leukemia nine months before Frankel first ran and Cecil died nine months after Frankel last ran. Strange thing, wasn't it?'

LAMMTARRA

(Derby, King George VI and Queen Elizabeth Diamond Stakes, Prix de l'Arc de Triomphe, 1995, plus one other win.)

'It's been forgotten, hasn't it, how sick Lammtarra was that spring? He almost died. Do you know, Sheikh Mohammed was telling me that he didn't do his first canter until 16 March and didn't do a serious piece of work until 11 April, and the Derby was on 10 June.

'It seemed quite impossible, to win the Derby having run just once as a two-year-old and not again until Epsom the next year. Lammtarra was the first horse since Grand Parade in 1919 to win on his seasonal reappearance. What a performance! He set a new course record, you know, and he lost a shoe coming out of the starting stalls.'

RED RUM

(Grand National 1973, 1974, 1977. Scottish Grand National 1974, plus 20 other wins.)

Knowledge of Red Rum's Grand National triumphs is taken for granted, as if it has seeped into the British public's bones.

It is the Cinderella tale of an unfashionably bred colt who was bought by former jump jockey Tim Molony for 400 guineas, and retained by him for 300 guineas after Red Rum was in a dead heat for first place with Curlicue in a five-furlong selling race at Aintree, the day before Foinavon won the Grand National. Later, he was bought by Donald 'Ginger' McCain, a feisty, opinionated character who trained his horses on the beach at Southport.

The bluffer will listen patiently to the endless retelling of the dramatic encounter between Red Rum and Crisp in the 1973 Grand National, when Red Rum, carrying 10st 5lb, plucked victory from the magnificent Crisp, carrying 12st. The villain that year, Red Rum was the hero the next, when it was his turn to carry 12st.

You will listen with rapt attention as the story reaches its 1977 climax with Red Rum's third victory, then remark casually, 'Personally, I've always found Sir Peter O'Sullevan's commentary a little disappointing. It's when O'Sullevan says, "He's coming up to the line to win it like a fresh horse," that I have trouble. With the greatest of respect, when a horse finishes the Grand National, it is not "a fresh horse".'

That should provoke a reaction, and therefore have served the bluffer's purpose.

SEA PIGEON

(Chester Cup 1977, 1978. Scottish Champion Hurdle 1977, 1978. Ebor Handicap 1979. Champion Hurdle 1980, 1981. Welsh Champion Hurdle 1980. Fighting Fifth Hurdle 1978, 1980, plus 27 other wins.)

His father was the great Sea-Bird, winner of the 1965 Derby. Sea Pigeon finished seventh in the 1973 Derby but blossomed as a dual-purpose horse in later life. As a nine-year-old, he won the Ebor Handicap at York when carrying 10st – no horse, certainly since 1930, has won the race when so old nor carrying such a big weight. Sea Pigeon then twice won the Champion Hurdle, aged 10 and 11. Only Hatton's Grace, who registered a hat-trick between 1949 and 1951, has won the race at such an advanced age.

Both Jonjo O'Neill, who rode Sea Pigeon in the Ebor and for the first of his Champion Hurdle successes, and John Francome, who rode him on the second occasion, regarded him as the best horse they ever rode, and they both rode some very good ones.

Over to the bluffer, ready as always to stir the mud. 'Wonderful horse on the Flat, even better over hurdles. Of course, Jonjo O'Neill came too soon on him in the 1979 Champion Hurdle, or he might have won it three times. He almost ballsed it up in the Ebor, too, dropped his hands and almost got caught by Donegal Prince. Still, fine rider, lovely chap, very successful trainer now, as you know.'

ALSO-RANS YOU NEED TO KNOW ABOUT

Just as films can be so awful that they attract a cult following, like *Attack of the 50 Ft. Woman* and *The Beast of Yucca Flats,* so can racehorses. Racing aficionados will have plenty to say about the great horses but the best of the worst may have escaped their attention. Here is a chance for the bluffer to shine!

AMRULLAH

Several things distinguished Amrullah (born 1980, died 2003) from countless other non-winners. The thing about Amrullah was that he was good enough to win races but preferred not to. In his prime, he beat some decent horses, such as Floyd and Hypnosis, but only on condition that at least one other horse was in front of him when they reached the winning post.

♔

He doesn't object to everything.
He likes biting and kicking.

Terry Thorn, owner of Amrullah

Amrullah didn't trouble the judge but was troublesome to Terry Thorn, his owner, and John Bridger, his trainer. One of Amrullah's victims was Gill Bridger, the trainer's wife, who emerged from one encounter with a broken arm. 'Don't worry,' Bridger told Thorn, 'it was a lovely clean break.'

When Amrullah retired, in 1992, his record stood at zero wins from 74 attempts. He could be accused of failing through want of trying.

QUIXALL CROSSETT

Six years after Amrullah retired, Quixall Crossett (born 1985, died 2006) passed his unenviable record and went on to lose 103 races out of 103 contested. Twice Quixall Crossett finished second, and six times he started at 500-1, a price rarely seen on a bookmaker's board.

Amrullah had talent but lacked temperament, whereas Quixall Crossett had neither, simply being very slow. Trained by Ted Caine, a North Yorkshire farmer, Quixall Crossett raced until he was 16 and had an active fan club – but many people came to feel that his retirement was overdue.

... AND RIDERS

Some very rude things are said about jockeys, not all of them by losing punters.

John Francome, six and a half times champion jump jockey (he tied with Peter Scudamore in the 1981/82 season) once declared, 'You could remove the brains from 90 per cent of jockeys and they would weigh the same.' That's unfair, although in a betting shop the word 'brainless' is heard quite often during the course of a race.

Jockeys are supposed to follow the instructions issued by the horse's trainer. Sometimes there aren't any instructions, sometimes they don't make sense, sometimes they can't be carried out, and sometimes the jockey just ignores them.

Former Yorkshire trainer Charles Booth, while being trailed for a TV documentary, watched in amazement as a leading jockey, who he had just told to hold his horse up, promptly booted the horse into the lead. Booth turned to the journalist: 'You heard me give the instructions. Was I talking ******* Chinese?'

After another unsatisfactory performance by a jockey named Wood, Booth asked him, 'Are you related to that

Russian jockey, Blokov?' Unsurprisingly, Booth has also remarked, 'I don't think there's a person in the country with a lower opinion of jockeys; overrated and overpaid.'

Opinions are influenced by outcomes. Winning a race is generally regarded as a good thing, reflecting well on the winning jockey, whereas losing a race is liable to provoke a search for riding errors.

♛

'The travelling band of certifiable madmen known as professional jockeys...'

Sue Mott, sports journalist

Bluffers need not let their limited – well, non-existent – knowledge of jockeys and jockeyship deter them. As with so much in horseracing, a subjective approach is common. John Whitley, a statistician, has long been contemptuous of those (almost everyone) with strong opinions about the relative merit of different jockeys based on their own subjective assessments. Whitley's company, Racing Research, produces annual jockeys' ratings based on a sophisticated computer analysis of how horses have performed for different riders. Fortunately for the bluffer, his own assessments, fragile of foundation but firm of conviction, are unlikely to cross Whitley's challenging path. They will merely have to cross swords with the subjective opinions of others.

A tentative foot in the water might take the form of, 'I

thought Johnson (as in Richard Johnson) gave that a good ride,' graduating to 'I'd like to have seen Spencer (as in Jamie Spencer) a bit nearer the pace,' and post-graduating to 'I thought McCoy (as in Tony McCoy, 20 times champion jumps jockey) gave that a dreadful ride.'

When asked why, a bit of bluster might be required.

FLAT JOCKEYS

Convention has it that a jockey is a small person who was advised by a teacher at school that, as he was no good at anything else, he might as well try to be a jockey.

Not all jockeys are small. Champion jockey Richard Hughes is 5ft 10in while George Baker, another leading rider, is 6ft. Granted, they are thin as celery, ride on tiny saddles and do not wear thick woolly jumpers. As a breed, Flat jockeys look badly in need of a big fried breakfast.

Amazingly, given their often long and frenetic working days and lack of steak and kidney pies, most of the sport's stars are approachable and good humoured, particularly in the winner's enclosure. Only a few follow in the Lester Piggott tradition, treating questions as a gourmet might treat a prison pudding (of which Lester had many following his conviction for tax evasion).

Flat jockeys keep going for decades. Hughes and Frankie Dettori are in their 40s while Piggott, a law unto himself, retired in 1985, when he was 50, then returned to win the 1990 Breeders' Cup Mile on Royal Academy and, aged 56, the 1992 2000 Guineas on Rodrigo De Triano. He finally retired at the age of 59.

APPRENTICES

On the Flat, learner riders are known as apprentices and are given a weight allowance as an incentive to trainers to give them rides. As the number of winners they ride goes up, the weight allowance goes down.

Capable apprentices can be in great demand and it is enjoyable and rewarding to try to spot promising young riders before their talent is widely noticed. Comments such as, 'That Robert Tart looks quite good,' and 'She looks good value for her 7lb claim,' should stand the bluffer in good stead.

JUMP JOCKEYS

Horses carry bigger weights in jump races so jockeys can be larger, without being fat. It is a dangerous sport, in which injuries are common. Jump jockeys are what is known as 'the salt of the earth', regularly displaying qualities such as courage, resilience, compassion, modesty and generally setting a fine example of what sportsmen should be like.

Tony McCoy, who was champion jumps jockey every year until he retired in 2015, and Richard Johnson, who was runner-up almost every year, set a fine example, emulated by others, of being fiercely competitive yet mutually supportive. A splendid bunch.

CONDITIONAL RIDERS

These are jump racing's version of apprentices. They are probably called conditional because, conditional on them being good enough and not complaining too much about broken bones, they will become proper jump jockeys.

AMATEUR RIDERS

Obvious, really. They aren't professional jockeys and don't get paid for riding. They do it for fun. In the old days, some were spectacularly bad which had a certain perverse fascination and provided opportunities for deploying expressions such as 'a sack of potatoes'.

Both on the Flat and over jumps, there are some races restricted to amateur riders, although over jumps, amateurs also ride regularly against professionals. The standard of riding has improved considerably over the last 30 years and amateurs now approach the sport in a more professional, and less cavalier, way. If their weight permits, they sometimes turn professional.

Many gain experience and ply their hobby at point-to-point meetings (*see* 'The Best of the Rest'). At these, vestiges of riding styles of old can still be seen and, in its fearless heyday, the Mackenzie & Selby's Hunter Chasers and Point-to-Pointers Annual was wondrously rude about the less able jockeys. 'The rider is a bold contender for worst rider of the year,' was a characteristic comment, as was, of horse and rider, 'Pulled up ninth fence, horse and rider appalling.'

WOMEN JOCKEYS (AND TRAINERS)

It seems unimaginable now but in 1966, Florence Nagle had to take legal action to force the Jockey Club to end their practice of refusing to issue training licences to women. Until then, women trainers were obliged to ask a male assistant or head lad to apply for a licence, with the yard's horses running in his name. In August 1966, when a horse called Pat won at Brighton, Norah Wilmot became the first licensed female trainer to train a winner under Jockey Club rules.

Women were still not allowed to ride in races, apart from a few ladies' point-to-point races and the historic Newmarket Town Plate, races not run under Jockey Club rules. In 1972, a series of a dozen Flat races for lady amateur riders was introduced. Meriel Tufnell won the first race, at Kempton on 6 May, on Scorched Earth.

Two years later, at Nottingham on 1 April 1974, amateur men and women raced against each other for the first time, with Linda Goodwill triumphing on Pee Mai. The following year, the Sex Discrimination Act obliged the Jockey Club to allow women to ride as professionals on the Flat and over jumps, causing much harrumphing among Club members.

Female jockeys still faced considerable resistance and hostility, and progress was slow. It wasn't until 1978 that Lorna Vincent, riding Pretty Cute, became the first woman to win a jumps race as a professional jockey. A month later, Karen Wiltshire followed her into the record books by becoming the first female professional jockey to ride a winner on the Flat, on The Goldstone.

The bluffer might care to file away these and other gender landmarks, with the names of Gay Kelleway and Alex Greaves, on the Flat, and of Charlotte Brew and Geraldine Rees, over jumps, being names to cherish and broadcast.

Kelleway was the first woman, and is still the only woman, to ride a winner at Royal Ascot – Sprowston Boy in the 1987 Queen Alexandra Stakes. Greaves became the first woman to win a Group 1 race in Britain when Ya Malak dead-heated in the 1997 Nunthorpe Stakes at York.

Brew was the first woman to ride in the Grand National, on Barony Fort in 1977, while Rees was the first to complete the course, on Cheers in 1982. All of these facts could come in very handy, possibly in a crossword.

♔

'Their bottoms are the wrong shape.'

Lester Piggott on female jockeys

Jenny Pitman was the first woman trainer to win the Grand National, with Corbiere in 1983, and the first to win the Cheltenham Gold Cup, thanks to Burrough Hill Lad in 1984. Pitman won both races again, the Gold Cup with Garrison Savannah in 1991 and the National with Royal Athlete in 1995. A feisty and prickly person, with enthusiastic admirers and equally enthusiastic critics, she once punched jockey Jamie Osborne for having hampered one of her horses. 'What can I say?' said Osborne. 'She's got a great left hook.' Former champion jump jockey John Francome remarked, 'The Alsatians in her yard would go around in pairs for protection.'

More recently, Henrietta Knight, a more placid soul,

trained Best Mate to win three Cheltenham Gold Cups in a row (2002 to 2004) plus the King George VI Chase (2002), which she also won the following year with another stable star, Edredon Bleu, who had won the Queen Mother Champion Chase at Cheltenham in 2000.

There have been other successful women trainers, mainly in jumps racing, including Mary Reveley and, currently, Venetia Williams, Sue Smith, Lucinda Russell and Rebecca Curtis.

Hayley Turner stands out as the most successful woman riding on the Flat in Britain. Joint champion apprentice in 2005, she rode 100 winners in 2008 and, in 2011, won the Group 1 July Cup on Dream Ahead and the Group 1 Nunthorpe Stakes on Margot Did. Cathy Gannon, Kirsty Milczarek and Shelley Birkett have also made their mark.

Over jumps, Lucy Alexander, champion conditional rider in 2013, is an exceptional talent while amateur riders Nina Carberry and Katie Walsh, based in Ireland and from legendary racing families, have both ridden winners at the Cheltenham Festival, Carberry four times and Walsh twice. In 2012, Walsh finished third in the Grand National, on Seabass.

It's a lot for a bluffer to take in but it's worth it. If you can't win a quiz armed with all that, there's something wrong with the quiz.

FANCY A FLUTTER?

I t is possible to go racing and not have a bet, just as it's possible to be in a strip club with your eyes closed. You don't have to bet, and a lot of people don't, but it's more fun watching a stripper with your eyes open and it's more fun watching a race when you've had a bet.

People love horses, and a lot of racegoers, as well as owners and trainers, go to see them parade and race rather than to bet on them, but most racegoers will have a bet, either tiny or huge, for interest or profit.

You can learn a lot about people's attitude to money from their betting behaviour. A rich man might be more upset about losing his £10 bet in a photo finish than a poor man his £2 wager on a horse that fell at the last fence, with the race won. Beware the man who keeps his money in a purse, agonises over his wallet, avoids ordering a round at the bar, and leads the conversation towards pensions. He would make a good racing companion, just as Kim Jong-un would make a good democrat.

As Sir Clement Freud, a talented loser, put it, 'If you mind losing more than you enjoy winning, do not bet.' It's well worth trying to be a good loser, as demonstrated by the unseemly sight of a bad one. At a racecourse, there are plenty of opportunities to practice. It's alright to cry, but best to wait until you get home before you do it.

There are small casual bettors and large serious ones, although many professional gamblers bet from home nowadays, while those at the racecourse are likely to be sitting in a private box in front of a computer, betting while a race takes place – 'in running'.

The bluffer will find betting a congenial pastime because punters, especially men (most punters are men), are prone to lie about their bets. Social anthropologist Kate Fox hit upon one of the reasons when she observed, 'In the unwritten etiquette of betting, £2 is a "lady's bet", and anything below a fiver casts serious doubt on the masculinity of the punter. The rule for males is: either don't bet on a race at all, or bet at least £5.'

'Without the involvement of money, it's largely just horses going round in circles.'

Dave Nevison, professional gambler

Fox was writing in 1999. Since then, racecourse bookmakers have helped masculinity along by imposing minimum stakes that are sometimes as high as £5. Whatever the stake, you will get to know whose betting stories can be believed and whose need to be taken with a tanker load of salt.

This is good news for bluffers, who will soon acquire a useful collection of betting responses, delivered with characteristic briskness and persuasiveness. Asked, 'Did you have that winner?' you will reply, modestly, 'Yes, but I lost my nerve and only had £200 on it. Still, at least I got 12-1.'

Later, asked, 'Have you had a bet in this race?' you will reply, 'No, to me the last winner was the standout bet today. I was amazed that he was 8-1. It's just a watching brief now.'

There are four mediums for betting at a racecourse. There are the bookmakers in the betting ring, standing at their pitches; there is the Tote; and there is the racecourse betting shop. The fourth is your own telephone, providing access to off-course bookmakers and betting exchanges, although using your phone for betting is likely to breach the terms and conditions of entry to the racecourse.

RACECOURSE BOOKMAKERS

Traditionally an integral part of the racing experience, bookmakers with names like Jolly Joe, loud check jackets and voices like foghorns used to shout the odds and hand out colourful cards as receipts while their clerks entered the bets in their ledgers and tic-tac men, standing on orange boxes, waved their white-gloved hands in signals of the trade, communicating changes in the horses' prices. The betting ring was a loud, busy and buzzy place.

Jolly Joe lives on (breaking news, he died in 2015, aged 88) but most but most of the old faces have gone and nowadays, apart from the big days, the betting ring is a less vibrant arena. At most meetings, there are fewer bookmakers, tic-tac men are extinct and the bookmakers' boards have gone digital, their chalk dispensed with. The ledgers have been replaced by laptops, the coloured cards by computer-generated paper tickets, and the big gamblers are elsewhere. The punters' hurried dash along the pitches in search of the best odds has lost its urgency, for there is less variation in the prices.

Nowadays, few, if any, bookmakers base their prices on their own opinions. Instead, they follow the off-course betting exchanges, led by Betfair. The market, once formed at the racecourse, is now shaped elsewhere.

Yet the age-long battle between bookmakers and punters goes on, and the changes have not all been for the worse. Both prices and customer service have improved. You will be treated politely and a dispute is unlikely, especially with details of your bet now printed on your receipt. Don't forget to check it.

HOW TO BET WITH A BOOKMAKER

There is nothing to be afraid of, apart from losing your money. Walk up and tell the bookmaker which horse you want to back. You used to say the horse's name, and still can, but racecourse bookmakers go by numbers now, so the horse's racecard number will do.

To back a horse to win, simply say '£4 win number 7, please,' provided the minimum stake is not £5. You will be given a ticket with details of your bet, including the odds and how much you will receive if the horse wins.

To back a horse each-way, say '£4 each-way number 7, please.' In effect, it is two bets – £4 to win and £4 for a place, making a total stake of £8. If you only want to spend £4, you need to bet £2 each-way.

Each-way is a simple and popular bet, complicated by the fact that whether or not a horse is placed, as well as the odds applied to the place part of the bet, vary according to the number of runners and whether or not the race is a handicap or non-handicap.

Place terms can vary and you should look at the bookmaker's board to see what they are. Standard terms are as follows.

Races with five to seven runners – one quarter the win odds for places one and two

Races with eight or more runners – one fifth the win odds for places one, two and three

Handicap races with 12 to 15 runners – one quarter the win odds for places one, two and three

Handicap races with 16 to 21 runners – one fifth the win odds for places one, two, three and four

Handicap races with 22 or more runners – one quarter the win odds for places one, two, three and four

Be vigilant when backing a horse each-way in a race where there is an odds-on favourite, particularly in non-handicap races. At the standard terms, there are often attractive bets to be struck in such races and bookmakers protect themselves, either by not offering each-way bets on the race, or by offering, say, one sixth or one seventh the win odds a place rather than one fifth the odds.

THE TOTE

You place your bets at Tote 'windows', giving the racecard number not the name of the horse you want to back.

There are two main differences between betting with a racecourse bookmaker and with the Tote. First, Tote bets are pool bets. All the money bet goes into a pool. The Tote takes a percentage and the balance is divided between the winning tickets. The odds are determined by the size of the pool and the number of winning tickets; the bigger the pool and the fewer winning tickets, the higher the dividend. When you place your bet, a screen will show the dividend for each horse at that moment but it might change by the time the race starts.

Second, as well as win and each-way bets, the Tote allows you to back a horse just for a place. There are a range of other bets. The main ones are:

Exacta Select the first and second horse to finish, in the correct order.

Trifecta Select the first, second and third horse, in the correct order.

Placepot Select a horse that is placed in each of the first six races.

Jackpot Select the winner of each of the first six races.

Scoop6 Select the winner of each of six selected Saturday races, with a consolation dividend if all your selections are placed, and a bonus to aim for if you have all six winners.

Not all of these 'exotic' bets are available on every race, nor every day. In the case of some bets, the pool is rolled forward if there are no winners. This sometimes produces very big pools for the Jackpot and Scoop6.

The Placepot is a very popular bet, providing an inexpensive interest throughout the afternoon (or, at least, until one of your selections is unplaced). You will be amazed at how many times five of your six selections are placed. It's almost a rule.

As with all these bets, you can have multiple combinations of selections, increasing your chance of winning but also increasing the cost, which can be pretty much as small or as large as you choose.

RACECOURSE BETTING SHOP

Very similar to any other betting shop. You write your bet on a betting slip and take it to the counter.

MOBILE PHONES

You can use your phone to bet with bookmakers or betting exchanges located elsewhere, and no doubt many racegoers do, but racecourses and those offering betting services on-course want you to bet with them. If you bet using your mobile phone you are probably breaking a condition of entry.

JUDGES AND STEWARDS AND WHY THEY'RE WRONG

It is the judge's job to decide which horse has won. He holds your fate and possibly your house in his hands, and eyes. Unfortunately, he is a man (usually a man) utterly indifferent to your welfare. He cares not whether you live in a palace or a poorhouse, and thinks nothing of turning you out of both. If you were in the gutter, he would probably evict you from there as well.

The judge studies a photograph of the finish, then announces, 'First, number 9'. You backed number 5, placed second. Does he care? You know the answer.

In the (good) old days, when technology was less advanced and judges more compassionate, desperately close finishes were declared to be dead-heats. The racing authorities regarded this as an admission of failure and Herculean efforts are now made to choose between the hairs on the noses of the candidates for victory.

Until 2008, the shortest official winning distance was a short head. This was deemed much too long and a shorter winning distance was introduced – a nose. It is only a matter of time before a nose is superseded by a short nose. Shortly after that, the word 'hair' can be expected to appear.

Once the judge has made you feel depressed, it is the stewards' job to intervene in order to raise, then dash, your hopes, thereby making you feel deeply depressed.

An incident during the closing stages of the final race of the day suggests that the winner caused interference to your runner-up, who was only beaten by a short head. The stewards call an inquiry. You wait, in nervous anticipation, while the stewards study replays, question the jockeys, and ask themselves whether, on the balance of probabilities, the interference improved the finishing position of the horse causing it? They are not satisfied that it did. An announcement is made. 'After the stewards' inquiry, the result stands.'

You have prepared yourself for this eventuality by climbing the stairs to the top of the grandstand. You throw yourself off. The judge and stewards set off home, looking forward to a pleasant dinner and a nice glass of Burgundy.

'There's nothing more irritating in a shop, when you're trying to sort out a winner or two, than constantly being forced by the volume of speech to overhear codswallop.'

Jeffrey Bernard, journalist

ARMCHAIR PUNTING

I f you are suffering from old age, you might remember John Rickman raising his trilby to viewers on ITV during the 1970s. That was his trademark. A bit of a bumbler, knowledgeable race fans were inclined to find him irritating while others found his affability and gentlemanly manners appealing. Most viewers just wanted to find the seven winners required to land the ITV Seven, or the six winners needed to win the ITV Six. It would have been hard enough if there had been an ITV One.

In those days, if you wanted to watch horseracing you had to go racing because TVs weren't allowed in betting shops and the one in your living room showed only what ITV and the BBC had to offer, a small percentage of all races.

Revolution arrived in 1987 when Satellite Information Services started broadcasting live pictures into betting shops. By then, Channel 4 had taken over horseracing coverage from ITV and, ultimately, from 2013, would have a monopoly of terrestrial TV coverage.

Another revolution in the early 2000s led to the creation of two dedicated racing channels, At The Races and Racing

UK. The former is free to subscribers to Sky Sports while the latter, which embraces the most prestigious racecourses, is a subscription channel.

What it all means is that, if you've got nothing better to do (you probably haven't), you can sit in your armchair and watch every single race, every day. How amazing is that? (Very amazing).

If that still leaves you at a loose end in the mornings, there is the Morning Line to watch on Channel 4 on Saturday mornings, and other things to watch on At The Races and Racing UK every morning. Don't worry about the evenings; there are currently an annual 363 twilight or evening fixtures to watch.

WATCHING AT HOME

If you know how to sit down and turn the TV on to the right channel, you've cracked it. That's all there is to it, although it's important to locate the button on your remote control called the 'mute' button.

The mute button greatly enhances the viewing experience. Not only does it spare you from listening to your least favourite presenters and pundits, it also means you can watch a race without hearing the commentator say, 'One's gone at that fence – it's the one you backed.' Silence may not be golden, but it's often preferable to the alternative.

You gather essentials around you – the *Racing Post,* a cup of tea and a chocolate biscuit, your glasses, your phone, the remote control. That just about covers it. You're good to go, although only as far as the armchair.

Racing is blessed with some fine commentators. Sir Peter O'Sullevan's unique tones are no longer to be heard (except on recordings), but commentators such as Simon Holt, Richard Hoiles, Stewart Machin, Mark Johnson, Ian Bartlett and several others are impressively accurate. You will discover your own preferences, and a bluffer will discover them and make them known quickly. It takes no time at all to remark, 'He's too loud for my taste, I must say. Sir Peter was never agitated. It was something he and I discussed several times.'

BETTING AT HOME

Having mastered the remote control, it remains only to master the telephone. Older-style telephone betting involves ringing a bookmaker and placing your bets by word of mouth. Mouths, however, are no longer needed, as smartphones, tablets and computers enable the sedentary, or non-sedentary, punter to bet online.

Online betting has totally eclipsed traditional telephone betting and, for tax reasons, all the major UK bookmakers have moved their online businesses off-shore, mainly to Gibraltar. Bet365, the biggest of them all, still employs over 2,600 staff in Stoke-on-Trent. Owned largely by the Coates family, Bet365 makes a fortune (pre-tax profit £214 million in 2013/14) part of which (£5 million in 2013/14) it spends on Stoke City Football Club, which the family also owns.

Launched in 2001, Bet365 is one of the great dot-com success stories. In 2013/14 almost three million active customers staked over £26 billion with the company, just over half of which is owned by joint chief executive Denise Coates CBE. If Mrs Coates wasn't already married, it might be worth proposing to her. The bluffer might try asking where she stands on bigamy.

BETTING SHOPS

Legalised in 1960 but on the basis that nothing must be done to stimulate the demand for gambling, early betting shops were tucked away, spartan, smoke-filled and uninviting. There were no window displays, no TV, no refreshments and barely any seats, since loitering was to be discouraged.

RA Butler, Home Secretary when the relevant Act was passed, later reflected that 'The House of Commons was so intent on making betting shops as sad as possible, in order not to deprave the young, that they ended up more like undertakers' premises.'

In those days, betting was dominated by horse and greyhound racing. It is very different now, when 7,877 of Britain's 9,108 betting shops are owned by four companies – William Hill, Ladbrokes, Coral and Betfred. In 2013, in William Hill's 2,432 shops, horseracing accounted for just 24 per cent of revenue and dog racing for nine per cent. Football supplied 13 per cent of the revenue but a massive 48 per cent came from Hill's 9,431 gaming machines.

Today, betting shops are bright, colourful, inviting places, with banks of TV screens, comfortable seats and refreshments, but many customers play roulette, blackjack, poker and slot games rather than back horses. In 2001 there were no gaming machines in betting shops; now there are over 34,000.

The racing industry, in its attempt to work out what would be best for itself, started by opposing machines, moved on to argue that racing should be given part of the profits from them, and now defends them for fear that further restrictions might result in betting shop closures that would prove damaging to racing's income.

The bluffer might wish to occupy higher moral ground and confine himself to watching and betting on horseracing while allowing himself the occasional critical comment on all things casino-like.

CUSTOMERS

As previously stated, most punters are men. There are several reasons for this, but one was neatly captured by a woman who explained, 'When a woman bets and loses, she thinks, "I wish I'd spent the money on a blouse." When a man bets and loses, he thinks, "I knew I should have backed the second favourite."'

Women tend to have better things to do than spend their afternoons losing money and are rarely heard encouraging their boyfriend or husband by saying, 'Go on, stick £100 on it. If it wins you can have me, as well.' So it's left largely to men to bravely ignore the fact that, behind the counter, three people are taking bets while only one is paying out.

The reputations of jockeys, trainers and stewards tend to be lower in betting shops than elsewhere, with their competence and integrity regularly questioned, particularly after a horse with a different name to the one on the customer's betting slip has been declared the winner.

Listening to post-mortems in Betfred can be irritating, as can the man ahead of you in the queue when you are trying to back a horse at Haydock and the race is about to start. The cashier has just said, 'You've got £6.30 to come back on that, Fred,' to which Fred replies, 'Is that all? Are you sure? I thought it was more.' A third voice intervenes. 'They're off at Haydock.'

You screw up your betting slip and walk back to your seat. Someone has taken it, and someone else has walked off with your *Racing Post*. You look up at the TV and watch the horse you would have backed romp home, at 12-1. A man next to you nudges your arm and shows you a betting slip. He's had £20 on the winner. 'Did you have that?' he says. 'I thought it was a certainty.'

TIPS AND SYSTEMS: YOU KNOW BEST

Horseracing is awash with tips and advice – some free, some to be paid for. The bluffer, being a novice without the time or knowledge to sort the wheat from the chaff, would do well to heed what the legendary gambler Barney Curley discovered, 'There was one way to ruin and that was to listen to people in racing.'

Most tips are not worth having, most systems don't work and the best thing to do (obviously, this tip might also not be worth having) is to rely on what you see for yourself when watching races and what the form book tells you.

A lot of punters believe that having a trainer, owner, jockey or work rider to advise them would be a passport to profit. Sadly, they are mistaken, as the paucity of trainers, owners and work riders who have become wealthy from betting demonstrates. Jockeys aren't allowed to bet, although it is not unknown for a jockey to have someone do it for him.

Overall, the diligent, well-informed punter is at least as well placed to bet successfully as most trainers and owners. Trainers know their own horses well and have private knowledge of a horse's well-being or otherwise that it would sometimes be useful to know, but they are generally less knowledgeable about their rivals' horses. The industrious form student often knows more about those.

There are genuine experts writing and broadcasting and, in time, the bluffer will identify them and pick their brains, perhaps presenting the contents as his own. In the meantime, all tips should be treated with caution and unsolicited invitations that arrive through the letter box, encouraging you to subscribe to a tipping service, should be treated with extreme caution. That is what your wastepaper bin is for.

With so many races to choose from, specialising is a good idea. You might, for instance, restrict yourself to betting only on Flat races or, within Flat racing, to races for horses older than two-year-olds. You could avoid handicap races, or bet only in January, giving yourself the rest of the year to pay off what you owe.

Good luck. You'll need it, although by now you should at least be able to bluff your way through.

'While the English are fond of their racing, I discovered the Irish can't live without it.'

Bill Barich, American writer

RACING ABROAD

The bluffer may or may not venture overseas but, in either case, he cherishes the ability to talk as if he were a regular visitor to the world's leading racing nations. France and Ireland, being the nearest, attract his immediate attention, although he is familiar, in word if not in deed, with Australia, Dubai, Japan and the USA.

AUSTRALIA

There are 700 racecourses to choose from. The bluffer will choose Flemington, near Melbourne, home of the Melbourne Cup Carnival, a four-day fiesta in early November climaxing with the Melbourne Cup itself, 'the race that stops a nation'.

It is a public holiday in Melbourne and it is party time, and dressing-up time – nuns and gorillas are popular. The race, over 3200 metres, is the world's most valuable handicap, with prize money totalling A$6.2 million (£3.4 million) in 2014.

For the bluffer, the essential facts are these. In 1993, Irish trainer Dermot Weld became the first overseas trainer to win the Cup, with Vintage Crop, who also won the 1992

Cesarewitch and the 1993 and 1994 Irish St Leger. Weld won the Melbourne Cup again, in 2002, with Media Puzzle.

Trainer Bart Cummings has won the Cup 12 times, while Makybe Diva won the race three times in a row from 2003 to 2005.

DUBAI

Sheikh Mohammed, the ruler of Dubai, has been a driving force in the internationalisation of horseracing. In 1992, he created the horseracing stable Godolphin, wintered and trained his best horses in Dubai and fired them off at top races around the world. Sheikh Mohammed's jockeys,

♛

The bluffer will, no doubt, be discussing all those trips to the Dubai World Cup.

notably Frankie Dettori, wore Godolphin's familiar royal blue colours. Within 10 years, Godolphin had won 100 Group 1 races in 11 countries.

In 1996, the first Dubai World Cup was staged at Nad Al Sheba, and won by Cigar, the American superstar. In 2004, what is now the Dubai World Cup Carnival was launched, providing several weeks of international races and, in 2010, Meydan racecourse was opened on the site of Nad Al Sheba.

The bluffer will, no doubt, be discussing all those trips to the Dubai World Cup, held at the end of March.

FRANCE

There are 148 racecourses in France, but you will confine your attention to the upper echelons of the sport. Early in the year, you may be seen at Cagnes-sur-Mer, near Nice, where English trainers were once regular visitors. In June, you will be at Chantilly for the Prix du Jockey Club and Prix de Diane; in August at Deauville, on the beach and in the casino as well at the racecourse, while the first weekend in October will find you, *naturellement*, at Longchamp, for the Prix de l'Arc de Triomphe.

First run in 1920, the Arc, as it is usually called, is the traditional climax of the European Flat season, won by many great horses. Although a 'pari-mutuel' (*see* Glossary) monopoly supplies plentiful prize money, many race meetings in France are poorly attended. Arc weekend is an exception, boosted by thousands of British race fans in Paris for a weekend of high-class racing and jollities.

GERMANY AND ITALY

Britain stages 33 Group 1 races, France 27, Germany and Italy seven each. The racing industries in both countries, particularly Italy, have been in serious difficulty in recent years.

If the bluffer had owned a horse suitable for a Group race in Italy (you didn't), he or she may have chosen to avoid it. The financial situation there was so dire that, in 2014, owners of horses that won Group races in Italy two years earlier were still waiting to receive their prize money.

A visit to Baden-Baden would be more tempting, to bathe in the spa waters, visit the Grand Casino, where Fyodor Dostoyevsky lost so much money that he had to write *The Gambler* to help pay for it, and watch the Grosser Preis von Baden, run in early September. It is a race many good horses have won, most recently Danedream, who won the race in 2011 before going on to win the Arc. The following year, having won the King George VI and Queen Elizabeth Stakes at Ascot, Danedream won the Grosser Preis von Baden again.

HONG KONG AND SINGAPORE

The Hong Kong Jockey Club has a monopoly of betting and, as there is a lot of it, racing at its two courses, Happy Valley and Sha Tin, is lavishly funded. The bluffer will be there, perhaps only in spirit, for the International Races in December, when four Group 1 races are headed by the HK$25 million (£2 million) Hong Kong Cup. Since it was first run in 1988, the Cup has been won three times by horses trained in Britain – First Island (1996), Falbrav (2003) and Snow Fairy (2010).

In May, you may want to visit Kranji racecourse in Singapore for their international races, the highlight being the S$3 million (£1.4 million) International Cup, twice won by British-trained runners, Endless Hall in 2001 and Grandera in 2002.

IRELAND

The Irish love racing and their enthusiasm produces a wonderfully engaging, egalitarian atmosphere at the 26 racecourses that are sustained by a population, north and south of the border, of only about 6.4 million people. Britain's population is around 63 million.

Despite the dominating presence of Coolmore's breeding and Flat racing operation, the passion of most Irish race fans is jump racing, with Punchestown and Leopardstown staging 25 of Ireland's 31 Grade 1 jump races, while the Curragh boasts 10 of the country's 12 Group 1 Flat races, including the five Irish Classics, matching the five English ones.

At Laytown, they race on the beach; at Killarney, against a magnificent mountain background; everywhere is fun. The racing Festivals offer an exciting if exhausting menu, including five days at Punchestown in April/May, four days at Killarney and seven at Galway in the summer, and seven more at Listowel in September. The bluffer will have some tales to tell.

JAPAN

Japan is a major racing and breeding location and, since 2010, all of Japan's Group races have been open to foreign runners. There are 23 Group 1 races but the Japan Cup, held at Toyko racecourse in November, with crowds of over 100,000 and prize money totalling 521 million yen (£3 million), remains the focus of European attention. Since it was first run in 1981, four English-trained horses have won the Japan Cup – Jupiter Island (1986), Singspiel (1996), Pilsudski (1997) and Alkaased (2005). In 2013, Blackstairmountain, trained in Ireland by Willie Mullins and ridden by Ruby Walsh, broke fresh ground and won over 65 million yen (£368,000) when winning the Grade 1 Nakayama Grand Jump.

The bluffer will also be conversant with the success of Japanese-trained horses overseas. Agnes World won the 1999 Prix de l'Abbaye at Longchamp and the following year's July Cup at Newmarket. Delta Blues won the 2006 Melbourne Cup and Victoire Pisa the 2011 Dubai World Cup. Several Japanese-trained horses have finished second in the Prix de l'Arc de Triomphe, namely El Condor Pasa in 1999, Nakayama Festa in 2010, and Orfevre in 2012 and 2013.

USA

The leader of the world in terms of Grade 1 races – there are 110 of them – but you might claim to make just three annual pilgrimages to the land where every racetrack is flat and left-handed and most races are on dirt.

In May, the Kentucky Derby at Churchill Downs in Louisville, first run in 1875, is not to be missed. A great carnival day, the infield full of partying students, the packed grandstand served with traditional mint juleps, the race is the most prestigious prize in the USA, with total prize money of $2.2 million (£1.5 million). 'The Run for the Roses' is the first leg of the Triple Crown, completed by the Preakness Stakes and Belmont Stakes and last won by Affirmed in 1978.

August means a month in Saratoga Springs, in upstate New York. Saratoga racecourse is the oldest in the USA, having opened in 1863. One of its founders was William Travers and the Travers Stakes is the pinnacle of an elegant meeting.

Finally, in October/November, to the Breeders' Cup, a two-day extravaganza with 13 Grade 1 races and $24.5 million (£15 million) in prize money, culminating in the $5 million (£2.5 million) Breeders' Cup Classic. 10 different racetracks have staged the Breeders' Cup since it was first run in 1984, but in recent years Santa Anita, a spectacularly beautiful racecourse in California, has become the favoured venue.

European horses are usually well represented, mainly in the races run on turf, but Arcangues, trained by André Fabre in France, was a shock winner of the Classic in 1993 and John Gosden, who trained in California for 10 years before moving to Newmarket, won with Raven's Pass in 2008.

There's no point in pretending that you know everything about horseracing – nobody does – but if you've got this far and you've absorbed at least a modicum of the information and advice contained within these pages, then you will almost certainly know more than 99 per cent of the rest of the human race about what horseracing is, why people enjoy it, and how you can pretend to know more about it than you do. What you now do with this information is up to you, but here's a suggestion: be confident about your newfound knowledge, see how far it takes you, but above all, have fun using it. You are now a fully fledged expert in the so-called 'sport of kings', one of humankind's oldest, noblest and most addictive pursuits. So go forth and punt.

Oh, and never, ever, imagine that you're on a 'hot streak' and that you can throw caution to the winds by betting everything you possess on a dead cert. The only dead cert is that you'll end up dead broke.

GLOSSARY*

Ante-post Arrangement under which punters can continue to bet after their death. Facility for losing six months before a race takes place.

Betting shop A bank specialising in deposits.

Blinkers The first act of desperation (to which might be added visor, cheekpieces, hood, tongue-tie).

Bloodstock agent Person who charges for persuading you to buy a horse for 10 times more than it will soon be worth.

Bluffer A person who other people believe knows what he or she is talking about.

Bookmaker Wealthy victim of repeated misfortune.

Change legs Undergo major surgery.

Change of scenery To remove a horse from one box and place it in another, 300 miles away, in the hope that it

* Most of the glossary items first appeared in the *Racing Post*. With thanks for permission to reproduce them.

might run faster.

Depression Small dip in racing surface. Chronic condition contracted in Ladbrokes.

Each-way Opportunity to lose twice in one bet.

Fall The sudden replacement of hope by despair.

Foot Part of leg used for stepping on nails or stones.

Form book Historical work, useful for predicting what will happen in the past.

Getting out stakes The final race of the day, offering punters the chance to leap from the frying pan into the fire.

Group race A race in which all the horses are triers. Such races make up only a small proportion of the racing programme.

Guineas Expensive pound. Part of drink needed after attending bloodstock sale.

Handicap A race in which horses of different abilities are given an equal chance of winning, to the delight of Betfred and the despair of their customers.

Heavy A description of the going, sometimes at racecourses, more often in William Hill's.

Hold up Keep a horse at the back of the field until a suitable pocket can be found for it.

Horsebox A vehicle that does five miles to the gallon,

specialising in trips to Perth.

Judge Official with no legal training or sense of justice, about to sentence you to a depressing fate.

Keen A horse that wants to go faster, but only for a while.

Lucky 15 An argument for strengthening the Trade Descriptions Act.

Nose Distance by which you have been beaten.

Over the top Ran badly in the autumn.

Overweight Excess fat carried by jockey.

Pen Item stolen from betting shop in order to make you feel that at least you've won something.

Photo-finish camera Equipment employed to prolong the agony.

Prayer Act of desperation, invariably treated with contempt.

Pull Run very hard at the start of a race in preparation for running very slowly at the end.

Punter Noble individual dedicated to hope in defiance of experience.

Queue What is in front of you when you are about to be just too late to back a 16-1 winner.

Replay Watch it go horribly wrong, again.

Saver Bet placed by punter in the belief that two bets will be less expensive than one.

Seller A race in which the winner is offered for sale to people who don't want it. A race in which horses that have no value are allotted one.

Setback Common disorder in which a racehorse retains the ability to generate bills but loses the ability to race.

Sore shins The result of a young racehorse putting one leg in front of another.

Spread betting An exciting introduction to the official receiver.

Starter Official who waits until the one you have backed is facing the wrong way, then pulls a lever.

Stayer A slow horse.

Steward Official employed to disabuse you of the belief that you have just backed your first winner in three months.

Talking horse A horse that runs fast on the gallops on Newmarket Heath but slowly on the Rowley Mile course.

Trainer Person employed to explain that your horse ran a lot better than it appeared to, despite finishing last, again.

Unlucky Horse that took part in a race but did not win it.

Vet (noun) Creature renowned for its enormous bill.

Vet (verb) To examine a horse with a view to discovering why you should not have bought it.

Win A spot of absent-mindedness by God.

Winning post White stick with a red circle on it situated in the wrong place.

Wintered well It's almost April and he's still alive.

DOWNLOADING THE APP WON'T COST YOU. NOT USING IT MIGHT.

Don't blow your money with dodgy tips or gut feelings. The Racing Post's live news, expert tips and animated predictions make light work of placing a well-informed bet. And with Ladbrokes and William Hill on board you don't have to leave the app to do so.

Pretty good for a freebie.

BET WITH YOUR HEAD

 m.racingpost.com

BLUFFING NOTES

Bluffing Notes

Bluffing Notes

Bluffing Notes

Bluffing Notes

THE *Bluffer's* ®GUIDE TO

BLUFFING

HOT OFF THE PRESS…
AND FREE!

Need to build your bluffing arsenal in a hurry?

**For instant expertise, arm yourself with
The Bluffer's Guide to Bluffing, filled with
flashes of brilliance from every current title
in the Bluffer's catalogue, from Wine to
Horseracing, Poetry to Food, Cricket to the
Quantum Universe, and more!**

Is there anything you *don't* know?

GET YOUR FREE EBOOK AT
BLUFFERS.COM/BLUFFFORFREE

MAXIMUM CREDIBILITY, MINIMUM EFFORT

A world of bluffing awaits: books,
gift sets and collections at bluffers.com

BEER	JAZZ
BOND	MANAGEMENT
CARS	OPERA
CATS	POETRY
CHOCOLATE	THE QUANTUM UNIVERSE
CRICKET	ROCK
CYCLING	RUGBY
DOGS	SEX
ETIQUETTE	SKIING
FISHING	SOCIAL MEDIA
FOOD	STAND-UP COMEDY
FOOTBALL	SURFING
GOLF	TENNIS
HIKING	UNIVERSITY
HORSERACING	WINE
INSIDER HOLLYWOOD	YOUR OWN BUSINESS